DEAR F*CKING MORON: 101 MORE RUDE LETTERS TO DONALD TRUMP

Copyright © 2019 Aldous J. Pennyfarthing

Published by:
Pennyfarthing & Dash Publishing, a wholly owned subsidiary of O'Reilly's Falafels and Loofahs Inc.

Aldous J. Pennyfarthing lives in the Pacific Northwest with his beloved wife, Penelope Middleton-Smythe, and their mutt terrier, Fiddlehead Stinktrousers. In contrast to Donald Trump's shambolic bearing, appearance, and comportment, Pennyfarthing is a natty hail-fellow-well-met and a gentleman. He resorts to the fatuous japery contained in this book out of a sincere love for country.

Also by Aldous J. Pennyfarthing:

Dear F*cking Lunatic: 101 Obscenely Rude Letters to Donald Trump

The Fierce, Fabulous (and Mostly Fictional) Adventures of Mike Ponce, America's First Gay Vice President

Author's note: If you're inclined to tweet excerpts of this book, or its cover, to @realDonaldTrump — or send them to the White House — well, I can't stop you.

Check out Pennyfarthing's Facebook page at Facebook.com/trumpworstpresident and his Twitter @Make_Trump_Cry.

This book is humbly dedicated to the Daily Kos community. Follow my posts at Daily Kos, and be sure to sign up!

INTRODUCTION

There's an Edenic paradise in the Bay of Bengal called North Sentinel Island.

You likely heard of it for the first time late last year when it made international headlines. A Christian missionary named John Allen Chau visited the island, which is banned to outsiders, in an effort to bring the word of God to its conspicuously "ungodly" inhabitants.

Of course, the island is closed to foreigners for several very good reasons, the most salient being: 1) the natives have no immunity to Western diseases, 2) their ancient, fragile culture could never hope to survive the influence of either well-meaning or ill-intentioned 21st century invaders, and 3) they will fucking *kill* you — a *lot* — if you come anywhere near them.

Chau blew through all these caveats because the Sentinelese had never read the Bible, and he decided this needed to be rectified, posthaste.

In the end, the Sentinelese filled him with a missionary zeal and a boundless, ineffable love for his fellow man — but, more importantly, they filled him with arrows.

And now he's dead.

Yes, what happened to him is tragic, but he wasn't really a missionary in the truest sense — he was a rapacious serpent trying to fuck with Eden by splicing his own peculiar brand of evangelical religion onto the Sentinelese people's unique 60,000-year-old culture. After all, the timid, enigmatic hunter-gatherers on North Sentinel Island may not have a written language; agriculture; the wheel; modern industry, medicine, or sanitation; hot-and-cold running water; Starbucks; or Netflix streaming, but they have something worth more than all the Starbucks or Netflix stock in the world: absolutely no awareness of Donald Trump whatsoever.

That ... is paradise.

Chau wasn't a good Christian trying to introduce a supposedly ignorant Stone Age culture to the saving grace of Jesus. He was a scoundrel attempting to sully their immaculate souls with the Fruit of the Knowledge of Donald Trump — which, it turns out, is simply a sweaty muskmelon cultivated for several months in the surpassingly moist under-bosom of Chris Christie.

In other words, he was a villain for the ages.

Personally, I'd love to be able to sashay along the pristine beaches of North Sentinel Island, blithely ignorant of the innu- ' merable depredations of Donald John Trump and the dozens of algae-green stink lines that follow him around giving him advice, but I drew the short straw and was born in Wisconsin in the mid-'60s, right around the time DJT was riding his magic bone spurs into a series of inexpert, soul-depleting handjobs in the second-least-squalid bathroom stall of the Atlantic City Long John Silver's.

And so now I have to write another book.

Because, you know, I'm a fucking patriot.

So if you don't know what motivates me, go ahead and read the first book in this series, *Dear F*cking Lunatic: 101 Obscenely Rude Letters to Donald Trump.* You'll find a more complete intro to Pennyfarthing therein.

But here's the thumbnail version:

Back in late-2017, Trump said something so monumentally stupid and dishonest (crazy, I know) that it awoke in me a rage demon that had somehow slumbered through two Bush presidencies and the perduring palpitations of Ann Coulter's Adam's apple. And as a regular blogger for the progressive/Democratic website Daily Kos, I figured it was time to power-spew some digital bile like never before.

And this is what gushed forth from my grubby keyboard:

Dear Fucking Lunatic,

I read with interest your recent interview with *The New York Times*. I couldn't get past the bit about your being the most popular visitor in the history of fucking *China*—a country that's only 2,238 years old, give or take.

Do you know how fucking insane you sound, you off-brand butt plug? That's like the geopolitical equivalent of "that stripper really likes me" — only 10,000 times crazier and less self-aware.

You are fucking exhausting. Every day is a natural experiment in determining how long 300 million people can resist coring out their own assholes with an ice auger. Every time I hear a snippet of your Queens-tinged banshee larynx farts, I want to crawl up my own ass with a Union Jack and claim my sigmoid colon for HRH Queen Elizabeth II.

We are fucking tired. As bad as we all thought your presidency would be when Putin got you elected, it's been inestimably worse.

You called a hostile, nuclear-armed head of state "short and fat." How the fuck does that help?

You accused a woman — a former friend, no less — of showing up at your resort bleeding from the face and begging to get in. You, *you, YOU* — the guy who looks like a Christmas haggis inexplicably brought to life by Frosty's magic hat — yes, *you* of all people said that.

You attempted — with evident fucking glee — to get 24 million people thrown off their health insurance.

You gave billions away to corporations and the already wealthy while *simultaneously telling struggling poor people that you were doing exactly the opposite.*

You endorsed a pedophile, praised brutal dictators, and defended *LITERAL FUCKING NAZIS!*

Ninety-nine percent of everything you say is either false, crazy, incoherent, just plain cruel, or a rancid paella of all four.

Oh, by the way, Puerto Rico is still FUBAR. You got yourself and your family billions in tax breaks for Christmas. What do they get? More paper towels?

Enough, enough, enough, *enough! For the love of God and all that is holy, good, and pure, would you please, finally and forever, shut your feculent KFC-hole until you have something valuable — or even marginally civil — to say?*

You are a fried dick sandwich with a side of schlongs. If chlamydia and gonorrhea had a son, you'd appoint him HHS secretary. You are a disgraceful, pustulant hot stew full of casuistry, godawful ideas, unintelligible non sequiturs, and malignant rage.

You are the perfect circus orangutan diaper from Plato's World of Forms.

So happy new year, Mr. Pr*sident. And fuck you forever.

Oh, and Pence, you oleaginous house ferret. Fuck you, too.

Sincerely,
Everyone

The post went viral, garnering tens of thousands of shares on Facebook and getting tweeted and retweeted by Chelsea Handler, Judd Apatow, and other members-in-good-standing of the liberal Hollywood cognoscenti.

But it appeared that Donald J. Trump, the bilious target of my bile-soaked screed, had not found it.

So I wrote an entire book full of letters, hoping he'd come to Jesus, so to speak.

But, alas, no. If anything, he got worse. Should I have expected a different outcome? After all, on a good day the guy is basically a spastic colon getting a Sriracha enema from a firehose, but even casual observers began to notice a crescendo of pique overwhelming the toddler occupant of 1600 Penn.

That crescendo continued to build, and build, and build, and pretty soon it made sense to wonder if forced White House naptimes were crucial to world peace and security.

Meanwhile, *Dear F*cking Lunatic* did pretty well for itself, earning me approximately TEN BILLION DOLLARS, give or take several billion.

More importantly, though, it served as a catharsis for all the refugees — i.e., members of the sane community — who've been brutally displaced from their former homes in the now-Bizarro States of America.

So here's a sequel. More letters, more ribaldry, more brawny epithets, and more acid-packed artillery aimed unswervingly at the irritated ocher asshole of our orangutan-in-chief.

Enjoy ...

◆ ◆ ◆

April 1, 2018

From the Desk of Aldous J. Pennyfarthing
To: Donald Trump, gibbering blatherskite

Dear Fucking Moron,

Dude!

We've been over this. Again and again. See my previous correspondence.

When I blasted my first splenetic missive into the blessed ether more than a year ago, you were merely the dipshit of the universe. Now, after suffering through another year and change of this, I'm convinced God unceremoniously sharted in his Spider-Man Underoos and hand-selected our universe, out of trillions upon trillions in the incomprehensibly vast multiverse, as the seedy little secret hamper in which to stash his embarrassing little accident.

You, my malodorous friend, are that accident.

So why oh why won't you let me help you?

My previous book could — and perhaps should — have been titled *Chicken Soup for the Necrotic, Rapidly Disintegrating Orange Twatwaffle's Vanishingly Small Whit of a Soul*, but I figured you'd never read anything without your name on it, so I had to compromise my grand artistic vision — at least until the clicker trainers in the Kremlin got you to consistently respond to "twatwaffle." (It's a carrot-and-stick approach, for the most part. Except the "stick" is an electric cattle prod custom-retrofit for morons' anuses and the "carrot" is deep-fried and made mostly of processed chicken skin.)

Anyway, now I have to do this all over again. I'm like Bruce Banner. I don't really *want* to be a rampaging rage beast, but I have no choice. Because you've *given* me no choice, you half-brained princeling.

So let's get started, shall we?

Pennyfarthing smash!

Love,
Pennyfarthing

April 3, 2018

- In an inscrutable reference to President Obama, Trump tweets, "Thank you to Rasmussen for the honest polling. Just hit 50%, which is higher than Cheatin' Obama at the same time in his Administration."

April 4, 2018

- Trump signs an order sending National Guard troops to the southern border to combat illegal immigration.

April 6, 2018

- The White House announces that Trump will skip the annual White House Correspondents' Dinner.

April 7, 2018

- A fire in Trump Tower kills a resident and injures six firefighters. The apartment did not have sprinklers, and it's later revealed that Trump had fought against a sprinkler requirement in New York City apartment buildings.
- Trump tweets out a defense of openly corrupt EPA administrator Scott Pruitt: "While Security spending was somewhat more than his predecessor, Scott Pruitt has received death threats because of his bold actions at EPA. Record clean Air & Water while saving USA Billions of Dollars. Rent was about market rate, travel expenses OK. Scott is doing a great job!"

From the Desk of Aldous J. Pennyfarthing
To: Donald Trump, clear and present diaper

Dear Fucking Moron,

Okay, listen up, gorilla tits.

Are you seriously trying to tell us that we have record clean air and water *because of Scott Fucking Pruitt?*

I know you love taking sole credit for decades of other people's hard work, but this is beyond the pale. I mean, you could have made a hog feces lagoon head of the EPA and it would have done a better job.

Also, and this is a serious question — just how openly corrupt does someone have to be to lose your confidence?

This guy — *this* guy — actually used $43,000 of taxpayer money to install a cone of silence in his office so people couldn't eavesdrop on his phone calls. I know it undermines veteran EPA employees' morale to overhear their director ordering sweet and sour panda from his manatee-leather office chair, but transparency in government is important. Can't he make his seedy backroom deals with fossil fuel companies in, I don't know, back rooms?

And as ironic as it is to have an EPA administrator flying everywhere on private jets (again, at taxpayer expense), that's nothing compared to getting a sweetheart deal on a Capitol Hill townhouse rental from a *fucking energy lobbyist!*

You seriously don't see a problem with that? No, of course you don't.

Let me put it this way. Imagine if you'd bribed a city official fair and square in order to erect one of your gaudy Brobdingnagian turd piles in Manhattan and then some other developer came along and gave that same government official a free condo to stay in because he wanted to construct a *good* building in that space.

Now do you see the conflict of interest?

Of course you do. Because it affects *you.*

Wow, this stuff is really easy when I can summon the courage to dive into your parking lot port-a-potty of a brain.

Why do I do this to myself?

Ugh.

Love,
Pennyfarthing

April 9, 2018

- After the FBI raids the office of Trump lawyer and "fixer" Michael Cohen, Trump calls it "an attack on our country in a true sense." He also says, "Why don't I just fire Mueller? Well, I think it's a disgrace what's going on. We'll see what happens. Many people have said you should fire him."

From the Desk of Aldous J. Pennyfarthing
To: Donald Trump, gangster doin' a bunch of gangster shit

Dear Fucking Moron,

At long last, I've figured out how to decode you.

"Some people" = You

"Many people" = You and Sean Hannity

"Everyone" = You, Sean Hannity, *Fox & Friends*, and the obstreperously flatulent machine elf you dreamed up last night after eating a 4-year-old box of Go-Gurt

And, yeah, it really bolsters our trust in you when you keep threatening the guy who's investigating your campaign. That *screams* "totally innocent."

Also, I would think an "attack on our country in a true sense" would be a hostile foreign power ratfucking our election in your favor and then you pretending it didn't happen.

So, yeah. Fire Mueller. Go ahead. I'm sure he hasn't kept any notes or anything. And if he has, they're probably just loose in the sweaty pocket of a coat he's had dry-cleaned 11 times by now. Because that's how decorated ex-Marines roll.

Don't worry about it. I mean, you're so totally pure and inno-cent I can barely stand to look at you.

Love,
Pennyfarthing

◆ ◆ ◆

April 12, 2018

- Trump creates a task force to look into the operations of the U.S. Postal Service. The announcement comes shortly after he tweets, "Only fools, or worse, are say-ing that our money losing Post Office makes money with Amazon. THEY LOSE A FORTUNE, and this will be changed. Also, our fully tax paying retailers are closing stores all over the country...not a level play-ing field!" Numerous observers speculate that he's sin-gled out Amazon because its owner, Jeff Bezos, also owns *The Washington Post*.

April 13, 2018

- Trump pardons Dick Cheney's former chief of staff, Scooter Libby, who had been convicted of obstruc-tion of justice and perjury.
- On Twitter, Trump calls James Comey an "untruth-ful slime ball" who should be prosecuted. "It was my great honor to fire James Comey!" he tweets.
- Trump reconsiders his decision to withdraw from the Trans-Pacific Partnership trade deal, which he once called a "disaster" being pushed by "special interests who want to rape our country."

April 15, 2018

- Trump again attacks James Comey, whose book, *A Higher Loyalty: Truth, Lies, And Leadership*, is scheduled to be released in days. "Unbelievably, James Comey states that Polls, where Crooked Hillary was leading, were a factor in the handling (stupidly) of the Clinton Email probe," Trump tweets.
- Trump tweets, "Comey throws AG Lynch 'under the bus!' Why can't we all find out what happened on the tarmac in the back of the plane with Wild Bill and Lynch? Was she promised a Supreme Court seat, or AG, in order to lay off Hillary. No golf and grandkids talk (give us all a break)!"

From the Desk of Aldous J. Pennyfarthing
To: Donald Trump, planetary facist-itis

Dear Fucking Moron,

Yeah, imagine a president trying to pressure the attorney general into dropping an investigation. What an outrage.

Seriously, dude, you have the self-awareness of a sea cucumber's asshole.

So it's beyond the pale if a woman's husband chats up the attorney general when she's under investigation, but you can hurl addlepated insults at your own AG nonstop like a feral toddler raised by prairie chickens. Sounds about right.

Meanwhile, the phony "witch hunt" just keeps finding witches. Come to think of it, it's really more like one of those canned hunts, where the dumb animals stand around on fenced lots gorging on piles of field corn while dutifully waiting to be shot in the head like one of Dick Cheney's manservants.

And, let's be honest, were it not for James Comey you'd be starring in a TLC reality show where you travel around Arkansas in an RV with Honey Boo Boo and the third-least-hygienic *Duck Dynasty* spawn.

Also, learn how to use quotation marks, FFS. How is it possible that your brain is this damaged yet still capable of telling your lungs how to breathe?

Love,
Pennyfarthing

April 17, 2018

- After UN Ambassador Nikki Haley announces sanctions against Russian companies that allegedly helped Syria with its chemical weapons program, White House economic adviser Larry Kudlow says, "She's doing a great job, she's a very effective ambassador. There might have been some momentary confusion about that." The remark prompts Haley to respond, "With all due respect, I don't get confused."

April 18, 2018

- Diplomatic officials state that Trump is working on the denuclearization of North Korea, but experts remain skeptical, and not just because he's a moron: "The surest way for the summit to end in disaster is if President Trump enters with the false belief that denuclearization of the Korean Peninsula means Kim Jong Un unilaterally surrendering his nuclear weapons," nuclear nonproliferation expert Vipin Narang tells *The Washington Post.*

April 19, 2018

- Former New York mayor and shrunken apple head Rudy Giuliani joins Trump's legal team

From the Desk of Aldous J. Pennyfarthing
To: Donald Trump, proud citizen of the CCCPee

Dear Fucking Moron,

So you snagged Giuliani, huh? What a coup.

How many Chuck E. Cheese Skee Ball tickets did you have to spend to lure him away from the animatronic jug band? Seriously, did you have to get permission from the Jizzmoppers Local 271 to let him work for you?

I don't know if you've seen him lately, but he looks like a popcorn ball that rolled under Grandma Dottie's bedroom couch six Christmases ago. You'd get better legal advice from a bath salts hallucination.

Then again, I've gotta hand it to you. He's the only lawyer on the planet who has to be viewed through 3-D glasses. So that's something, anyway.

And this quote!

"I'm doing it because I hope we can negotiate an end to this for the good of the country and because I have high regard for the president and for Bob Mueller."

Sure. Good luck with that. What's he going to negotiate with? Charm? He's what coffee breath would be if it were conjured into human form. If you shoved a pair of chattering novelty teeth up a longshoreman's asshole and said *that* was your lawyer, at least you'd have a puncher's chance. And no one but the longshoreman would know the difference.

Good luck with the "negotiations." I'm sure you'll be off the hook and happily wanking it to *Hannah Montana* reruns in no time.

Love,
Pennyfarthing

April 21, 2018

- Trump attacks *New York Times* reporter Maggie Haberman on Twitter and insists Michael Cohen will never flip: "The New York Times and a third rate reporter named Maggie Haberman, known as a Crooked H flunkie who I don't speak to and have nothing to do with, are going out of their way to destroy Michael Cohen and his relationship with me in the hope that he will 'flip.' They use.... non-existent 'sources' and a drunk/drugged up loser who hates Michael, a fine person with a wonderful family."

April 22, 2018

- Trump claims that North Korea has agreed to denuclearize. It hasn't.

April 24, 2018

- Trump says that if Iran restarts its nuclear program it will "have bigger problems than they ever had before."

April 25, 2018

- Rep. Kristi Noem (R-S.D.) says Trump once told her his dream is to have his face on Mount Rushmore. "I started laughing," she said. "He wasn't laughing, so he was totally serious."

From the Desk of Aldous J. Pennyfarthing
To: Donald Trump, risible rockhead

Dear Fucking Moron,

I think there's a pretty long waiting list for Mount Rushmore, you gormless cockwomble.

It's sorted by priority, and right now you're slotted somewhere between Herbert Hoover's face and Millard Fillmore's pendulous, 218-year-old scrotum. Pray that you don't fall any further.

But here's a tip: Most sentient humans, when a fellow traveler laughs directly in their face, do a peremptory sanity check. It's an instinct that apparently evolved so people don't jump off cliffs thinking they can fly. Or push the country off a cliff thinking they can be president.

By the way, exactly whose face do you think they should

sandblast off Mount Rushmore so they can stick your repugnant titian drool-spigot on there? I know you have a great relationship with "the blacks," but do you really think you should displace Lincoln? Washington and Jefferson are two of our most important Founding Fathers, and Teddy Roosevelt was instrumental in creating our national park system. I'm not sure that calling women "Horseface" on Twitter while pinching a loaf in your Emperor Palpatine jammies is going to get you there. But maybe. I'm not really sure who decides these things.

Maybe you should settle for that prison tattoo of your name on Billy Bob's skull. You'll have a lot more chances to look at that anyway.

Love,
Pennyfarthing

◆ ◆ ◆

April 26, 2018

- Trump neglects to get his wife a 48th birthday present, saying, "I got her a beautiful card. You know I'm very busy to be running out looking for a present."
- Ronny Jackson withdraws as Trump's choice to head the Veterans Administration in the wake of several accusations, including that he crashed a government car while driving drunk.
- Mike Pompeo is confirmed as secretary of state.
- In a *Fox & Friends* interview, Trump once again betrays his wounded feelings over his popular vote loss.

◆ ◆ ◆

From the Desk of Aldous J. Pennyfarthing
To: Donald Trump, whinging cocknose

Dear Fucking Moron,

So I know how you feel here, man:

> "Remember, we won the election. And we won it easily. You know, a lot of people say 'Oh, it was close.' And by the way, they also like to always talk about Electoral College. Well, it's an election based on the Electoral College. I would rather have a popular election, but it's a totally different campaign. It's as though you're running — if you're a runner, you're practicing for the 100-yard dash as opposed to the 1-mile."

I remember once in third grade when we were all playing dodgeball. It was shirts versus skins. (You probably know it as "brownshirts versus skinheads," but that's not important right now.)

Anyway, the teacher called me out because I was on the shirts team and one of the balls grazed my Jimmie J.J. Walker "Dyno-mite!!!" shirt. I mean, how is that fair? THE SKINS WEREN'T WEARING SHIRTS! So I still don't think it should have counted. At all. Come on!

We won the game, of course, but man oh man, that still pisses me off! I bring it up pretty much every day. I go up to strangers at Old Country Buffet and bitterly complain about it before sneaking some double-deep-fried cauliflower bites off their plates. Then I drive to Perkins, order a 12-pound banana nut muffin with a brick mason's wheelbarrow full of I Can't Believe It's Not Butter, and repeat the process. This goes on all day because BULLSHIT!

I mean, what kind of ridiculous, chickenshit call *was* that? I know we won, but still. We could have won by *way more* maybe.

Yeah, it was a long time ago, but I still think that teacher should have had his nuts pressed into whimsical star shapes in a Play-Doh Fun Factory.

I'm not sure why I'm bringing this up, honestly.

What were we talking about?

Love,
Pennyfarthing

◆ ◆ ◆

April 27, 2018

- Trump tweets, "KOREAN WAR TO END! The United States, and all of its GREAT people, should be very proud of what is now taking place in Korea!"

April 28, 2018

- Trump holds a rally in Michigan at which he says Kanye West "gets it," threatens that he knows things about Sen. Jon Tester, and says "we've got to win the House" or there will be "a lot of unhappy people."

◆ ◆ ◆

April 30, 2018

- South Korean President Moon Jae-in sucks up to Trump, saying he should win the Nobel Peace Prize.
- Porn star Stormy Daniels, whom Trump paid $130,000 in hush money, files a defamation suit against the pr*sident.

May 1, 2018

- Dr. Harold Bornstein, Trump's longtime doctor, claims three men connected to Trump raided his office and took Trump's records. The incident allegedly occurred two days after Bornstein told a newspaper he had prescribed Trump a hair-growth medicine.

◆ ◆ ◆

From the Desk of Aldous J. Pennyfarthing
To: Donald Trump, Lex Luthor's freshly shorn nard-cozy

Dear Fucking Moron,

We *know* you're bald, motherfucker. We all saw that video of you walking up to Air Force One looking like a cross between Doc Brown and a helmetless Darth Vader.

This is like Tony Soprano roughing up his doctor so she won't reveal that she told him to eat more cruciferous vegetables.

Or is there something else you want kept hidden? Do you have a slightly less intelligent parasitic twin who does all your tweeting for you? It would explain a lot, honestly. Is the CIA harvesting your STDs for a secret biological warfare program?

Why does everything you do have to be so fucking mobstery? It's just a bald pate. You should be more worried about what's going on *inside* your head, because no miracle of modern medicine can fix that.

Love,
Pennyfarthing

May 2, 2018

- News outlets report that Trump plans to replace Ty Cobb, the lawyer advising him on the Mueller probe, with veteran attorney Emmet Flood, who represented Bill Clinton during the Whitewater affair.

May 4, 2018

- After Rudy Giuliani reveals that Trump reimbursed Michael Cohen for the $130,000 hush payment Cohen made to porn star Stormy Daniels, Trump says, "Rudy is a great guy, but he just started a day ago. He'll get his facts straight."
- Trump ends immigration protections for 57,000 Hondurans who have lived in the U.S. for nearly 20 years.
- Trump speaks at the NRA's national convention, declaring, "Your Second Amendment rights are under siege. But they will never, ever be under siege as long as I'm your president."

May 5, 2018

- UK's *The Observer* reports that Trump aides hired an Israeli private intelligence firm to dig up dirt on Obama administration officials who helped negotiate the Iran nuclear deal.
- Several media outlets report that John McCain doesn't want Trump to attend his funeral.

From the Desk of Aldous J. Pennyfarthing
To: Donald Trump, worthless bag of bone spurs

Dear Fucking Moron,

Hope your fee-fees aren't hurt too badly by John McCain's funeral snub. But, seriously, what did you expect? McCain was an honorable public servant and a brave ex-POW with a storied and celebrated military career. You being at his funeral would be like playing the Benny Hill theme over the closing credits of *Saving Private Ryan*.

Really, though, he likes presidents whose ass fat *wasn't* captured in the drain of a hot tub.

Still, this is concerning. Usually events like these are bipartisan love-fests — which just goes to show that political disagreements and grudges can be transcended through a shared spirit of patriotism and bonhomie. That is, unless you're you. Think of how repugnant the pr*sident of the United States has to be to be explicitly disinvited from the funeral of a senator from his *own party*.

By the way, apropos of nothing, I looked up "bone spurs" on the Mayo Clinic website (don't waste your time going there; it has nothing to do with condiment-heavy ham salad sandwiches):

> The main cause of bone spurs is the joint damage associated with osteoarthritis. Most bone spurs cause no symptoms and can go undetected for years. They might not require treatment. If treatment is needed, it depends on where spurs are located and how they affect your health.

This is what kept you out of Vietnam? A symptom-free condition caused by osteoarthritis? Why didn't you just tell the draft board you couldn't serve because you were too busy underlining your stories in the *TV Guide*?

Jesus Christ, you are the phoniest tough guy on the planet. I'd have felt safer patrolling the Mekong Delta with an effervescently flatulent Teletubbie than with your fat ass. Luckily I didn't get drafted because, well, I was 9 when the war ended. And I had cataracts and some really nasty-looking liver spots on my tiny freak-show hands.

Love,
Pennyfarthing

May 7, 2018

- Melania Trump launches her Be Best campaign, which will focus in part on promoting responsible social media use and "encouraging positive social, emotional, and physical habits."
- Trump asks Congress to cut $15 billion in previously approved spending, including for the Children's Health Insurance Program.

From the Desk of Aldous J. Pennyfarthing
To: Donald Trump, marital piss

Dear Fucking Moron,

Poor Melania.

I'm sure she thought her life would be nothing but Tiffany bracelets and Manhattan dinner parties until the day she discovered your purpling carcass slathered in McNugget sauces, awkwardly propped, arms and legs akimbo, against your golden loo. And now she has to do all this tedious "first lady" horseshit. Will it never stop?

Of course, it goes without saying that if Melania wants to encourage "positive social, emotional, and physical habits," she should start with the wanton headcheese she shares her bed with.

Wait, does she still sleep with you, or has she started sleeping in the hall closet with a can of hairspray and a butane lighter like all your paramours eventually do?

You should tweet about this. Throw in a "Crooked Hillary" or two, maybe a "Little Adam Schitt." Your supporters can't spot irony anyway. Or Beefaroni stains on tank tops, apparently.

And what the fuck does "Be Best" mean? It's clearly missing a definite article. Personally, I think immigrants should learn our language before they come to this country to marry dickless silver-spoon cretins who are terminally redolent of special sauce and primal shame.

And it's just precious that your wife is launching an anti-child-bullying campaign on the same day that you propose slashing funds for impoverished children's health care. I love her campaign, but can she change the name to "Be Dust" just to make it a smidge more accurate?

Of course, most of us are convinced that Melania is actually trolling you 24/7, and an anti-bullying campaign is a great way to do that.

Then again, if she's *not* trolling you, you've clearly married a tone-deaf idiot.

So your choices are 1) your wife is dumber than a bale of back hair or 2) she fucking *hates* you.

Then again, both could be true.

Love,
Pennyfarthing

28

May 8, 2018

- Trump pulls the U.S. out of the Iran nuclear deal, opening the door to new sanctions against the country. "This was a horrible one-sided deal that should have never, ever been made," he claims. His advisers had earlier insisted that the deal was working and Iran remained in compliance.

May 9, 2018

- Trump tweets, "The Fake News is working overtime. Just reported that, despite the tremendous success we are having with the economy & all things else, 91% of the Network News about me is negative (Fake). Why do we work so hard in working with the media when it is corrupt? Take away credentials?"

May 10, 2018

- Several media outlets report that Homeland Security Kirstjen Nielsen nearly resigned after Trump berated her during a Cabinet meeting.

May 11, 2018

- In an interview with NPR, White House Chief of Staff John Kelly says Trump is "embarrassed" by Robert

Mueller's Russia investigation.

May 13, 2018

- Trump tweets, "North Korea has announced that they will dismantle Nuclear Test Site this month, ahead of the big Summit Meeting on June 12th. Thank you, a very smart and gracious gesture!"
- Citing an anonymous source, *The Washington Post* reports that Trump complains about the FBI's raid on Michael Cohen as often as "20 times a day."

From the Desk of Aldous J. Pennyfarthing
To: Donald Trump, OCDipshit

Dear Fucking Moron,

Do you need your binky, dear? I know it's very upsetting that they broke into your friend's treehouse and stole the secret list of girls you like, but that's how it goes sometimes.

Can I make you some chicken soup with stars? Maybe get you a Fruit Roll-Up?

Michael is still your friend, right? I don't think there's any way he would tattle. You treat him very nicely. Sure, maybe you shouldn't have made fun of him in front of the whole class those 800 times, but he's a nice boy. He won't say anything.

But, honey, you need to let this go. You've got lots of homework to do. Your big social studies project on North Korea is almost due.

Maybe we should put you on Ritalin. Are you taking anything else right now besides your lead paint chips, whippits, and airplane glue? I want to make sure nothing is contraindicated.

Get some sleep, bug. It's a school night, and you have a real big day ahead of you tomorrow.

Love,
Pennyfarthing

◆ ◆ ◆

May 15, 2018

- Trump eliminates the White House's top cyber adviser position.

◆ ◆ ◆

May 16, 2018

- In his annual financial disclosure, Trump acknowledges he paid Michael Cohen between $100,000 and $250,000, a portion of which is widely believed to be reimbursement for Stormy Daniels' hush money payment.
- Referring to some undocumented immigrants, Trump says, "These aren't people. These are animals, and we're taking them out of the country at a rate that's never happened before."
- SNL cast member Pete Davidson claims that Trump faked a phone call about his book sales when he hosted the show: "He was, like, weird all week. He, like, faked a phone call during the table read. Right as we started he was like, 'Hello.' He goes, 'Fantastic. Okay, great.' And then he hung up and he goes, 'Hey, everybody! My book just went No. 1!' I swear on my life. We were all, like, 'Yo, that phone didn't ring.'"

From the Desk of Aldous J. Pennyfarthing
To: Donald Trump, best-swelling blighter

Dear Fucking Moron,

Sigh.

You know, usually insensate evil isn't this fucking goofy.

I guess the closest we've ever come to this would be John Wayne Gacy in the clown outfit, but that doesn't quite capture your *je ne sais quoi*.

You're more like if Uday Hussein had done a prop comedy bit on a 1985 episode of *Star Search* and then showed it to every political dissident he ever tortured.

First of all, why would you ever brag about your book sales? You don't write those books, and everyone knows it. Well, everyone who can read, anyway.

I've seen your tweets. You sound like a 4-year-old stroke victim writing fan letters to Heinrich Himmler. There's no way you wrote *any* of those books. To write a book you generally have to sit still for more than five minutes at a time and engage in linear thought, and your head is basically just a bingo ball cage full of *Mein Kampf* quotes.

Just stop already. You're not a best-selling author. Because you're not an author. You stuck your name on someone else's work and pretended you accomplished something.

Gee, that sounds familiar, huh?

Love,
Pennyfarthing

◆ ◆ ◆

May 17, 2018

- On the first anniversary of Robert Mueller's appointment as special counsel, Trump tweets, "Congratulations America, we are now into the second year of the greatest Witch Hunt in American History."
- Gina Haspel is confirmed as CIA director. Among the senators opposing her confirmation is former POW and torture victim John McCain, who states, "Her refusal to acknowledge torture's immorality is disqualifying."
- Footage of Bill Gates is released in which he revealed that he twice had to explain to Trump the difference between HIV and HPV.

May 20, 2018

- Trump invents a spy that the FBI supposedly placed in his campaign and demands the Department of Justice investigate: "I hereby demand, and will do so officially tomorrow, that the Department of Justice look into whether or not the FBI/DOJ infiltrated or surveilled the Trump Campaign for Political Purposes - and if any such demands or requests were made by people within the Obama Administration!"

May 22, 2018

- Citing "space limitations," the EPA prevents reporters from CNN and the Associated Press from attending an event where EPA head Scott Pruitt is speaking.

May 23, 2018

- In an interview with the BBC, Steve Bannon says Martin Luther King Jr. would have been proud of Trump.

◆ ◆ ◆

May 24, 2018

- Trump cancels his summit with North Korea's Kim Jong Un.

◆ ◆ ◆

May 28, 2018

- Trump uses Memorial Day as an opportunity to brag about himself.

◆ ◆ ◆

From the Desk of Aldous J. Pennyfarthing
To: Donald Trump, jingoistic jizzcock

Dear Fucking Moron,

What the fuck is this, you pendulant sack of Goodwill dildos?

> "Happy Memorial Day! Those who died for our great country would be very happy and proud at how well our country is doing today. Best economy in decades, lowest unemployment numbers for Blacks and Hispanics EVER (& women in 18years), rebuilding our Military and so much more. Nice!"

I've spent thousands of days on this forlorn azure marble inexorably hurtling through a cosmic backwater in the outer spiral arm of a wholly unremarkable galaxy — one that swirls deliberately, like a languid latte cloud, among countless billions of sister galaxies — and it's been an incredible ride, all things considered. But it still felt somehow empty ... incomplete ... bereft.

Until today.

Thank you, thank you, *thank you.*

Because until now I'd never had occasion to seriously ponder what ghost vomit looks like.

Now that that thought has been extracted from my quavering, gelatinous cortex with a Fiskars landscape edger and a pair of marginally sanitized "Operator" tweezers, I can die, in quiet equanimity, knowing I've experienced everything there is worth experiencing.

Anyway, I'm so glad you gave all those brave American soldiers who are currently beholding the eternal beatific vision, permeated mind and soul in everlasting Elysian wonder, a big fat fucking thrill today. But you know what they could really use? An invite to the Oval Office and a platter full of oily, lukewarm fast-food french fries.

Could you somehow make that happen? I mean, you have a direct line to the afterlife, right?

Love,
Pennyfarthing

May 29, 2018

- A Harvard study concludes that 4,645 deaths can be linked to Hurricane Maria and its aftermath.

May 30, 2018

- "Melania Trump" tweets that she's actually at the White House working for the American people and not in a shallow grave somewhere outside of Palm Beach.

◆ ◆ ◆

From the Desk of Aldous J. Pennyfarthing
To: Donald Trump, psycho-bobblehead

Dear Fucking Moron,

So no one has seen Melania in 20 days. Do you think she's joined Sea Org to escape the suffocating cultlike environment of the Trump White House?

You know, if she were at the bottom of an old, abandoned well in the creepy Victorian lair of a Delaware serial killer who kept screaming "it puts the lotion in the basket!" I think most of us would be like, "Oh, good for her! She's moving on with her life. Meeting new people. And she finally *left* that asshole!"

But no such luck for Rapunzel, I'm afraid.

And, no, this tweet isn't fooling anyone, BTK:

> "I see the media is working overtime speculating where I am & what I'm doing. Rest assured, I'm here at the @WhiteHouse w my family, feeling great, & working hard on behalf of children & the American people!"

Yeah, nice tweet, "Melania." Way to cover your tracks. How did you get into your wife's Twitter account, anyway? Was her password something really easy to guess, like "ForTheLastFuckingTimeKeepThatDisgustingWithered-HorrorshowOfAPenisOutOfMe"?

I'm not saying you murdered Melania with a Mike Pence-branded butt plug in the Lincoln bedroom after she caught you jerking off to your own rally speeches in an Eva Braun costume and then stashed her dismembered body in a series of progressively twee American Girl doll heads that you keep in quart-sized Zip-Loc bags underneath the Oval Office floorboards, but I'm not *not* saying it, either.

Anyway, she'll turn up — when she realizes 20 days isn't nearly enough time for you to eat yourself into a coma.

Love,
Pennyfarthing

May 31, 2018

- Trump announces that he plans to pardon conservative polemicist Dinesh D'Souza, who pleaded guilty in 2014 to campaign finance violations.

June 1, 2018

- Trump tells the media his summit with Kim Jong Un is back on.

June 4, 2018

- Trump rescinds his invitation to the Super Bowl champion Philadelphia Eagles after several members of the team say they plan on skipping the event in response to Trump's attacks on players who kneel dur-

ing the national anthem.
- Trump claims he has the "absolute right" to pardon himself.

From the Desk of Aldous J. Pennyfarthing
To: Donald Trump, weasel-dicked dick-weasel

Dear Fucking Moron,

Seriously? This?

> "As has been stated by numerous legal scholars, I have the absolute right to PARDON myself, but why would I do that when I have done nothing wrong?"

Okay, you can try, but you'll go blind!

Sorry, I misread that. I guess I need glasses. For, uh ... some reason.

So according your theory, you could kill as many reporters, congressmembers, and ex-wives as you want so long as you sign pardons faster than you pull the trigger. So if you had some kind of mechanized rubber stamp device attached to a Gatling gun, you'd be home free.

For some reason I don't think that's what the Founding Fathers had in mind.

Anyway, you won't be in office forever, and if you do pardon yourself you'll be staked out 24/7. And the chance that you *don't* eventually fuck a billy goat at the end of a four-day Adderall bacchanal or kill a hobo over a disputed can of Libby's cling peach slices is approximately nil. So watch yourself.

OJ didn't go to prison for murder ... but he went away eventually.

Don't get too cocky.

By the way, if you've done "nothing wrong," why are you even bringing up pardons?

I don't just randomly tweet, "For your information, haters, I have the ANTIDOTE to lethal squirrel monkey herpes, but I don't have the disease, so why would I ever take this viscous, light-amber elixir that I've clearly researched exhaustively?"

You really should play professional poker, man, because you have *zero* tells. It's uncanny, really.

Love,
Pennyfarthing

June 5, 2018

- After withdrawing his White House invitation to the Super Bowl champion Philadelphia Eagles, Trump hosts a "Celebrate America" event on the South Lawn. During the event, Trump attempts to sing "God Bless America" but appears to forget the words.

June 6, 2018

- Trump claims that the Coast Guard was forced to rescue thousands of people during Hurricane Harvey because "people went out in their boats to watch the hurricane."

◆ ◆ ◆

From the Desk of Aldous J. Pennyfarthing

To: Donald Trump, twatfaced fuckbucket

Dear Fucking Moron,

What ...

The ...

Ever ...

Living ...

Fuck ...

Are ...

You ...

Talking ...

About ...

You ...

Scurfy ...

Shit-for-brains ...

Troglodyte ...

?

This simply didn't happen ... because it's basically impossible.

For some reason, you insist on assuming that *everyone's* brain is perpetually awash in hagfish slime.

First of all, here's you:

> "I think this year the Coast Guard, maybe in terms of increased branding — the brand of the Coast Guard has been something incredible what's happened. Saved 16,000 people, many of them in Texas, for whatever reason that is. People went out in their

boats to watch the hurricane. That didn't work out too well. That didn't work out too well."

And here's a timely dispatch from ~~Politifact.com~~ Planet Earth:

"The Houston Chronicle said in a news story posted later the same day that law enforcement 'first responders' were baffled by Trump's boating claim which, the story said, nobody could explain."

I swear, if you weren't (allegedly) president of the United States, you'd be sharing a holding cell with the guy they caught jerking off at the Bethesda Dunkin' Donuts in a Sailor Moon costume.

I mean, what the fuckity-fucking-fuck? Where do these brain farts come from? If you went on *Celebrity Jeopardy* they'd have to match you up against Scott Baio and a damp sack of macerated assholes, just to keep it interesting.

I wish I could just make up stories and expect people pay rapt attention to them. That could be fun.

"Hey, NASA shrank Buzz Aldrin to the size of a pistachio nut and shot him up my ass with an aerosol Reddi Wip can! I'm president! Can you believe it?"

Love,
Pennyfarthing

◆ ◆ ◆

June 7, 2018

- Asked whether he's ready for his summit with North Korean leader Kim Jong Un, Trump says, "I think I'm very well prepared. I don't think I have to prepare very much. This isn't a question of preparation, it's a question of whether or not people want it to happen, and we'll know that very quickly."

- *The New York Times* reports that the White House Council of Economic Advisers has concluded Trump's tariffs will hurt economic growth in the U.S.

June 9, 2018

- During a press conference at the G7 summit, Trump says Russia should be readmitted to the group of nations. Trump also blames President Obama for Russia's invasion of Crimea, rather than ... Russia.
- After departing the G7 summit, Trump withdraws support for a joint statement signed by all the group's members and lashes out at Canadian Prime Minister Justin Trudeau, tweeting, "PM Justin Trudeau of Canada acted so meek and mild during our @G7 meetings only to give a news conference after I left saying that, 'US Tariffs were kind of insulting' and he 'will not be pushed around.' Very dishonest & weak."

June 10, 2018

- Trump trade adviser Peter Navarro piles onto Justin Trudeau during a Fox News interview, remarking, "There's a special place in hell for any foreign leader that engages in bad faith diplomacy with President Donald J. Trump and then tries to stab him in the back on the way out the door."
- Politico reports that Trump regularly rips up official documents, requiring aides to tape them back together to prevent the administration from violating the Presidential Records Act.

From the Desk of Aldous J. Pennyfarthing
To: Donald Trump, all the crazy in the world

Dear Fucking Moron,

Why can't you at least try to be a normal boy?

You are so, so, *so* deeply weird.

Did you happen to read this Politico piece?

> "Armed with rolls of clear Scotch tape, [Solomon] Lartey and his colleagues would sift through large piles of shredded paper and put them back together, he said, 'like a jigsaw puzzle.' Sometimes the papers would just be split down the middle, but other times they would be torn into pieces so small they looked like confetti.

> "It was a painstaking process that was the result of a clash between legal requirements to preserve White House records and President Donald Trump's odd and enduring habit of ripping up papers when he's done with them — what some people described as his unofficial 'filing system.'"

As much as I'd like to rip up anything having to do with your "presidency," this just isn't done. Why? Because you're an adult who, through some bewildering, arabesque cosmic error, became president of the United States.

I guess some of the sting will be taken out of this when I'm in Oslo accepting my Nobel Prize for proving that trillions upon trillions of parallel universes exist, and we're definitely in the most fucked-up one.

As I will concisely explain, with an infinite number of universes and an infinite expanse of time, everything has to happen eventually. But this? I thought it would take at least another 6 billion years and 100 googolplex universes.

But here we are. Not only are you president, but you spend every last moment in the Oval Office acting like a chronically bored zoo ape.

God help us.

Love,
Pennyfarthing

June 12, 2018

- Trump and Kim Jong Un sign a toothless statement promising to work toward the denuclearization of the Korean peninsula. Most experts see the document as purely symbolic.
- A January 2018 *Wall Street Journal* article surfaces in which it's revealed that Vladimir Putin once advised Trump to end joint military exercises with South Korea — a concession Trump promised Kim Jong Un during the U.S.-North Korea summit.

From the Desk of Aldous J. Pennyfarthing
To: Donald Trump, Russian asshat

Dear Fucking Moron,

Well done, Harry Treasoner!

Jesus Fish-Slappin' Christ. Come on! I mean, when it comes to Putin, you're basically Blofeld's cat. And this is just what comes out in the media! I pray to God there isn't video of Putin flashing a laser pointer around the room while you frantically try to catch the red dot.

Clearly, when Putin asks you to jump, you say, "How high? ... And on the hypersensitive, ductile nutsack of which vital American ally?"

The only difference between you and a bona fide Russian agent is the agent wouldn't be so *fucking obvious*. Maybe you should watch a few episodes of *Get Smart* so you can glean a few tips.

Where did all this Russia love come from, anyway? Were you gestated in a Siberian bearskin full of Stoli? Did a piece of Sputnik crash into Queens and get lodged in your skull?

At least 325 million patriotic Americans would like to know.

Love,
Pennyfarthing

June 13, 2018

- Two Norwegian knuckleheads nominate Trump for the Nobel Peace Prize.
- After returning from his summit with Kim Jong Un, Trump assures the world that the North Korean nuclear threat is completely over.

From the Desk of Aldous J. Pennyfarthing
To: Donald Trump, Kim Jong's goon

Dear Fucking Moron,

Okay, just one question. Does your completely made-up fantasy universe have an urgent care facility where you can get evaluated for concussion-like symptoms? Because nothing you say in this tweet is even tangentially connected to reality:

"Just landed - a long trip, but everybody can now feel much safer than the day I took office. There is no longer a Nuclear Threat from North Korea. Meeting with Kim Jong Un was an interesting and very positive experience. North Korea has great potential for the future!"

Oh, *great job*, Chairman Maw! Is Kim Jong Un's head in your carry-on or something? Because the "agreement" you signed with him might as well have been written on your clammy little lemur hand for all the good it's going to do.

So you gave up joint U.S.-South Korean military exercises, gave North Korea a long-coveted propaganda coup, and saluted a North Korean general. If Obama had done any of that, Sean Hannity's rectum would have burned through his Sunday Dockers like a lit bag of white phosphorous. I'm just surprised Kim didn't trick you into eating a bug.

And what did you get in return? A signature on a nonbinding piece of paper. Say, maybe you should ask your ex-wives how much that's really worth.

But I'm glad you're closer to collecting a complete set of brutal authoritarian dictator bubblegum cards. That's something at least. Right?

Love,
Pennyfarthing

June 14, 2018

- New York state attorney general Barbara Underwood sues Trump and his foundation and asks a judge to dissolve the charity. Underwood says her office's investigation revealed "repeated and willful self-dealing" as well as illegal political coordination.

- Trump's former chief economic adviser Gary Cohn says Trump's trade war is a terrible idea: "If you end up with a tariff battle, you will end up with price inflation, and you could end up with consumer debt. Those are all historic ingredients for an economic slowdown."

June 15, 2018

- Trump imposes tariffs on billions of dollars of Chinese goods, stating, "In light of China's theft of intellectual property and technology and its other unfair trade practices, the United States will implement a 25 percent tariff on $50 billion of goods from China that contain industrially significant technologies."
- In a *Fox & Friends* interview and then later in an impromptu news conference outside the White House, Trump makes several easily refuted and very stupid claims, including, "It's in the agreement [with North Korea]. It says he will denuclearize. ... I signed an agreement where we get everything, everything."
- After Buzzfeed reports that Trump told G7 leaders Crimea is Russian because everyone there speaks Russian, the hosts of a Russian state media program declare, "Crimea is ours, Trump is ours!"

June 18, 2018

- DHS Secretary Kirstjen Nielsen says, "We do not have a policy of separating families at the border" — even though the administration has a policy of separating families at the border.

- Trump tries to shift blame for his administration's family-separation policy to Democrats, tweeting, "It is the Democrats fault for being weak and ineffective with Boarder [sic] Security and Crime. Tell them to start thinking about the people devastated by Crime coming from illegal immigration. Change the laws!

From the Desk of Aldous J. Pennyfarthing
To: The American People
cc: Donald Goat-Fucking Trump

Dear Voters, et al.,

This is the price of voter apathy. This is what happens when good people sit on their hands and think they have no voice — that their vote doesn't matter:

Kids are snatched away from their parents and thrown in cages.

If we don't get out in droves upon droves next November to kneecap this shart-slurping, retrograde prick who minces about like King Fuckwit in the West Wing, listening to nauseating encomiums from his fawning shit brigade while kids languish in concentration camps, we deserve to lose our democracy.

How much quasi-Nazi B.S. do we have to bear witness to in order to make the next presidential election a historic repudiation of our dictator-in-waiting?

My fear is that when 2020 comes around, too many of us will forget what's happening now.

But we can't. We just can't. Whatever happens, we need to be just as angry then as we are today. November 3, 2020, will be the most important day of the year, by far. Fuck you, Christmas. Our holiday comes early next year.

We have to remember every outrage of the past two years. Every. One.

Remember family separation

Remember DACA

Remember Puerto Rico

Remember Parkland

Remember Charlottesville

Remember Obamacare sabotage

Remember the Paris Climate Accord

Remember the Iran nuclear deal

Remember "shithole countries"

Remember the travel ban

Remember the tax scam

Remember Roy Moore

Remember Joe Arpaio

Remember the baiting — and then praising — of Kim Jong Un

Remember the erosion of our best alliances

Remember the denials of Russian election interference

Remember the attacks on the rule of law

Remember Stormy Daniels

Remember the Keystone Pipeline

Remember "clean coal"

Remember Scott Pruitt

Remember Betsy DeVos

Remember our transgender soldiers, who were able to serve our country with pride before Trump decided he didn't want to mistakenly grope the wrong private's privates

Remember the national anthem protests and our shitgibbon-in-chief's shameful response to the same

Remember every outrage

Remember all of it, put it in a box if you must, and unwrap it in November 2020. But take some time once in a while to let it sear your gut — enough so that you can't even think about staying home when your one opportunity to send a meaningful fuck-you to this heedless medieval ass-tart comes around.

Get registered, get an ID if it's required, do whatever the fuck you have to do to make this devil pay for his inhumanity. And do it now.

If you're in a safe blue state, vote anyway. Drive your friends and neighbors to vote. We have to send a clear message. We want a tsunami, not a ripple.

If you're in a safe red state and like the status quo just fine, fuck you — there are no safe red states anymore. We're challenging them everywhere, up and down the ballot.

If someone has an R next to their name, bzzzz, sorry. Thanks for playing. His or her opportunity to stop this slow-motion car wreck has long since gone the way of Crystal Pepsi and Zubaz.

And if someone has a "*rump" in their name, flush long and fuck-ing hard.

If you're mad as a hornet now because of what's happening at the border, make sure you're just as mad in November 2020, and put your anger — finally and fatefully — to good use.

No excuses. None.

Our democracy depends on you.

Love,
Pennyfarthing

June 20, 2018

- The AP reports that the Trump administration has set up "tender age" facilities to detain children who have been stolen from their parents at the southern border.
- Facing fierce political pressure, Trump signs an executive order ending his policy of separating children from their families at the U.S.-Mexico border. He had earlier said he couldn't resolve the problem through an executive order.

June 21, 2018

- Trump tweets, "'I REALLY DON'T CARE, DO U?' written on the back of Melania's jacket, refers to the Fake News Media. Melania has learned how dishonest they are, and she truly no longer cares!"

June 26, 2018

- After the Supreme Court upholds Trump's travel ban, which is aimed at several Muslim-majority countries, the pr*sident solemnly tweets, "SUPREME COURT UPHOLDS TRUMP TRAVEL BAN. Wow!"

- The Congressional Budget Office concludes that the national debt is set to explode and will reach 100 percent of GDP within a decade, in large part because of the Republican tax cut promoted and signed by Trump.
- For at least the second time, Trump claims U.S. Steel is building six new facilities that U.S. Steel knows nothing about.

◆ ◆ ◆

From the Desk of Aldous J. Pennyfarthing
To: Donald Trump, steelhead lout

Dear Fucking Moron,

Wait, is our country getting six new U.S. Steel facilities or are you getting six new steel plates in your head? Because this tumescent mound of happy horseshit definitely ain't happening:

> "U.S. Steel just announced they're expanding or building six new facilities."

> "The head of U.S. Steel called me the other day, and he said, 'We're opening up six major facilities and expanding facilities that have never been expanded.' They haven't been opened in many, many years."

Well, you might want to ask U.S. Steel about this because they have no idea what the fuck you're talking about, Pepe.

Anyway, here's what *Washington Post* fact-checker Glenn Kessler had to say about your fantasy factories:

> "President Trump has a tendency to cite conversations that did not occur quite the way he describes them — if they took place at all."

Wait, let's just stop there and let that soak in. See, this is why I don't take Ambien before I go to bed. I'm afraid I might sleepwalk to Oscar Mayer and stick my face in the pimiento loaf slicer. Because my subconscious is a *lot* smarter than I am, apparently.

He continued:

> "So we were a bit suspicious when he mentioned a phone conversation with Dave Burritt, chief executive of U.S. Steel.

> "Burritt did take part in a roundtable in March at the White House, and in May the president appeared to reference that meeting.

> "But then, on June 20, the conversation became a phone call. On June 26, Trump suggested the news was disclosed in a public announcement.

> "One would think this would be easy to clear up. But the White House did not respond to a query. Burritt also did not respond to an email from The Fact Checker asking him to confirm the conversation.

> "Meghan M. Cox, U.S. Steel's spokeswoman, simply offered this response: 'To answer your question, we post all of our major operational announcements to our website and report them on earnings calls. Our most recent one pertained to our Granite City 'A' blast furnace restart.'"

In other words, you invented — out of whole cloth — six entirely fictional U.S. Steel factories. That's just great. You've given new hope to thousands of at-risk Oompa-Loompas. You should be quite proud, Lieutenant Squirrel Shit. Say, now might be a good time to check if that pencil lead you shoved in your ear in kindergarten has reached your hippocampus yet.

Love,
Pennyfarthing

June 27, 2018

- Supreme Court Justice Anthony Kennedy announces his retirement.

June 29, 2018

- Trump's top economic adviser, Larry Kudlow, tells Fox Business Network that the deficit is decreasing "rapidly." It's not.
- Trump tweets, "Before going any further today, I want to address the horrific shooting that took place yesterday at the Capital Gazette newsroom in Annapolis, Maryland. This attack shocked the conscience of our Nation, and filled our hearts with grief..."

From the Desk of Aldous J. Pennyfarthing
To: Donald Trump, enemy of humanity

Dear Fucking Moron,

Yeah, where would anyone ever get the idea to murder journalists? I mean, they're only the enemy of the people. Still, *someone* had to point that out. How else would people who never, ever read newspapers know?

And you're not fooling anyone, by the way. I'll believe you wrote that tweet when Jesus Christ returns to Earth and gets a gig selling irregular MAGA swag and discount corn dog fryers on QVC. It doesn't sound like you at all. It sounds more like a human being with empathy. It would have been far more convincing if you'd attached an unflattering photo of Ted Cruz's wife, or written it in all caps, or said "conscious" instead of "conscience." You know, like a real president.

So maybe just sit this one out, okay? For some reason people tend not to appreciate condolences from assholes who hate them.

Love,
Pennyfarthing

June 30, 2018

- Three days after tweeting this ... "HOUSE REPUBLICANS SHOULD PASS THE STRONG BUT FAIR IMMIGRATION BILL, KNOWN AS GOODLATTE II, IN THEIR AFTERNOON VOTE TODAY, EVEN THOUGH THE DEMS WON'T LET IT PASS IN THE SENATE. PASSAGE WILL SHOW THAT WE WANT STRONG BORDERS & SECURITY WHILE THE DEMS WANT OPEN BORDERS = CRIME. WIN!" ... Trump tweets this ... "I never pushed the Republicans in the House to vote for the Immigration Bill, either GOODLATTE 1 or 2, because it could never have gotten enough Democrats as long as there is the 60 vote threshold. I released many prior to the vote knowing we need more Republicans to win in Nov."

July 1, 2018

- After some Democrats call for an end to ICE, Trump says, "You know ICE, these are the guys that go in and take MS-13, and they take them out. Because they're much tougher than MS-13, like by a factor of 10. And these are the ones — you get rid of ICE, you're going to have a country that you're going to be afraid to walk out of your house."
- *Howard Stern Show* regular "Stuttering John" Melendez reveals that he successfully phone-pranked Trump by posing as Sen. Bob Menendez, and says he talked to the pr*sident on Air Force One.

July 3, 2018

- Trump sends out a tweet meant to reassure his followers that he's *a really smart person* who writes *extremely* well.

From the Desk of Aldous J. Pennyfarthing
To: Donald Trump, illiterate wankface

Dear Fucking Moron,

What's this now?

> "After having written many best selling books, and somewhat priding myself on my ability to write, it should be noted that the Fake News constantly likes to pour over my tweets looking for a mistake. I capitalize certain words only for emphasis, not b/c they should be capitalized!"

*pore

Jesus Christ

Love,
Pennyfarthing

◆ ◆ ◆

July 5, 2018

- A Quinnipiac poll reveals that just 49 percent of Americans think Trump is a racist.
- Trump announces the resignation of openly corrupt EPA administrator Scott Pruitt.
- Trump, who has been accused of sexual assault by numerous women, mocks the #MeToo movement while attempting to ridicule Sen. Elizabeth Warren: "Let's say I'm debating Pocahontas, right? I promise you I'll do this. I will take, you know, those little kits they sell on television for $2 ... and in the middle of the debate ... we will take that little kit, but we have to do it gently because we're in the MeToo generation ... we will slowly toss it hoping it doesn't hit her ... and we will say, 'I will give you a million dollars to your favorite charity paid for by Trump if you take the test and it shows you're an Indian.'"

◆ ◆ ◆

July 6, 2018

- Former coal lobbyist Andrew Wheeler is named acting EPA administrator.

◆ ◆ ◆

July 7, 2018

- Trump tweets, "Twitter is getting rid of fake accounts at a record pace. Will that include the Failing New York Times and propaganda machine for Amazon, the Washington Post, who constantly quote anonymous sources that, in my opinion, don't exist - They will both be out of business in 7 years!"
- After Secretary of State Mike Pompeo hails the progress he made during talks with North Korea, North Korea contradicts his rosy assessment, saying, "The U.S. side came up only with its unilateral and gangster-like demand for denuclearization."

July 9, 2018

- Trump nominates Brett "Bart O'Kavanaugh" Kavanaugh to the Supreme Court.
- A BBC documentary series reports on Trump's behavior toward young women at parties during the '80s and '90s. One interviewee says of Trump, "This guy was like a predator in action. The next day or days after we would hear about it, he would brag about it to his friends and it would get around that he scored. Maybe one or two girls at a time, which is what he loved to do."

From the Desk of Aldous J. Pennyfarthing
To: Donald Trump, Chris Hansen's perviest houseguest

Dear Fucking Moron,

"Donald Trump is a disgusting, concupiscent diaper full of ogre shit with a diseased lab monkey brain who preys on vulnerable underage girls" will likely not be the lead headline from your upcoming visit to the UK, but it probably should be.

Because this, from a BBC investigation, via Vice News:

> "Trump's behavior toward younger women was described by a man who attended the same parties as like that of a 'predator.'
>
> "One of the women, Barbara Pilling, said she met Trump at a party in New York in the late 1980s while she was a young model. She alleged that then-businessman Trump asked her how old she was and approved when she said she was 17, allegedly responding: 'Oh, great. So you're not too old and not too young. That's just great.'
>
> "Pilling said she was not the youngest girl at the party, claiming there were girls as young as 14 attending. 'I felt I was in the presence of a shark,' Pilling said, describing Trump."

Goddamn you. Just when I was starting to keep food down again.

Of course, I've been at several wild parties with tweenage girls. They came running up to me, gave me a big hug, and said, "Thanks for the dolphin poster, Uncle Aldous!"

Okay, that's a lie. I never went to any of those parties. Why? Because I'm a middle-aged man, and hanging out at parties with teenage girls is really dull and *fucking inappropriate*. What the fuck is wrong with you, Dumbert Dumbert?

I just hate that every time I sit down to read the paper these days I have to fold Dear Abby into an air-sickness bag first.

Okay, that's another lie. I read newspapers on my computer now. Do you have one of those? It's that secret box where you hide all your illegal porn.

Jesus Christ, grow the fuck up.

Love,
Pennyfarthing

◆ ◆ ◆

July 11, 2018

- Trump kicks off the NATO summit by claiming Germany "is a captive of Russia." It just goes downhill from there.
- During Trump's introductory remarks at the NATO summit, White House Chief of Staff John Kelly appears to cringe as Trump insults U.S. ally Germany. Press Secretary Sarah Huckabee Sanders later claims that Kelly "was displeased because he was expecting a full breakfast and there were only pastries and cheese."

◆ ◆ ◆

From the Desk of Aldous J. Pennyfarthing
To: Donald Trump, ficken dummer Esel

Dear Fucking Moron,

Holy shit, you are a special kind of stupid. After you were born your mother should have kept the placenta and used you to fertilize her azaleas.

You realize it's not 1942, right? Germany is our *friend*. They're Kool and the Gang, man. Cool-de-la. Hitler has left the building.

Have you been playing too much Castle Wolfenstein or something? Because, for the life of me, I can't understand why you're antagonizing one of our best, most trusted allies. There are some very fine people in Germany, believe me.

You should take a trip there sometime. Maybe write an article for Frommer's. Something about how the Munich prostitute urine has a piquant, oaky flavor that stands in stark contrast to the insouciant floral overtones of Moscow hooker piss.

And, seriously, if your press secretary is going to blatantly gaslight us, at least ask her to put some shoulder into it. John Kelly looked like he wanted to flay the wet orange infield tarp off your Stay-Puft endoskeleton with his mind because he was *hangry*? Try again, dipshit.

If that story is true, he shouldn't be White House chief of staff. He should be riding a bus to Branson with a bunch of surly octogenarians who are screaming at the driver to stop at Cracker Barrel.

Again, Germany: good; Russia: bad

Need that edited down a bit? Maybe printed on two separate flashcards? More colorful pictures? Or do you just need your name in there somewhere?

Fuck the FDA for ever regulating codeine. I'ma need to make about two-dozen popsicles from that shit and suck on 'em for days while listening to whale songs.

Love,
Pennyfarthing

July 13, 2018

- Robert Mueller indicts 12 Russian intelligence officers for election interference.
- During a meeting with Queen Elizabeth II, Trump violates royal protocol several times, including by keeping her waiting for 15 minutes.

- Trump calls an interview he gave Britain's *Sun* newspaper, in which he criticized British Prime Minister Theresa May, "fake news." The newspaper later reveals that the interview was recorded.

◆ ◆ ◆

From the Desk of Aldous J. Pennyfarthing
To: Donald Trump, audio gaga

Dear Fucking Moron,

Can we all agree that things you say that are recorded on audio and then transcribed and published 100 percent in context are not "fake news"? Gotta say, you're making hereditary monarchy look better every day.

I mean, I get why you want to live in your own made-up universe. Join the club! In my fantasy universe, Mr. T is president, and he's just defeated Vladimir Putin in Thunderdome for the right to rule our post-apocalyptic hellscape. And for some reason Alexandria Ocasio-Cortez insists I ride in her Batgirl-cycle sidecar. Who am I to argue? And now we're on our way to Vegas, which happens to be the seat of the post-apocalyptic government, as well as the only place in the Western hemisphere that still has a Wetzel's Pretzels. It's a pretty grim life, but we do have an old tube TV and a VCR — though the only movies that survived the nuclear holocaust are *Short Circuit 2* and the extended director's cut of *Hope Floats*. But the *best part* is that we can generate all the electricity we need by dangling a cheese-encrusted Quarter Pounder wrapper in front of you as you desperately try to catch up to it on a stationary bike.

Yes, that world is so, *so* much better than this one.

Also, stop embarrassing us in front of the fucking Queen. Jesus Effing Christ.

Love,
Pennyfarthing

◆ ◆ ◆

July 15, 2018

- Trump calls the European Union a foe of the United States, citing "what they do to us on trade."

◆ ◆ ◆

July 16, 2018

- The Treasury Department announces that certain nonprofit groups, including the NRA, will no longer be required to give a list of donors to the IRS.
- At a joint press conference with Vladimir Putin, Trump sides with the Russian president over his own intelligence agencies on the question of Russian election meddling. "My people came to me, Dan Coats came to me, some others, they said they think it's Russia," Trump said. "I have President Putin. He just said it's not Russia. I will say this, I don't see any reason why it would be."

◆ ◆ ◆

From the Desk of Aldous J. Pennyfarthing
To: Donald Trump, vodka lemonhead

Dear Fucking Moron,

You.

Are.

A.

Fucking.

Traitor.

Full stop.

Love,
Pennyfarthing

◆ ◆ ◆

July 17, 2018

- In the face of almost universal derision, Trump attempts to walk back his defense of Russia over election meddling, saying, "The sentence should have been: 'I don't see any reason why I wouldn't' or 'why it wouldn't be Russia.' Sort of a double negative."
- A Russian state TV host says, "When Trump says our relations are bad because of American foolishness and stupidity, he really smells like an agent of the Kremlin."

◆ ◆ ◆

July 18, 2018

- Asked whether Russia is still targeting the U.S., Trump says "no."
- White House press secretary Sarah Huckabee Sanders claims Trump did not say Russia is not targeting the U.S.: "The president ... was saying 'no' to answering questions. The president and his administration are working very hard to make sure that Russia is unable to meddle in our elections as they have done in the past."
- *The New York Times* reports that Trump received

"very clear" intel two weeks before his inauguration proving that Vladimir Putin personally ordered cyberattacks against the U.S. in order to influence the 2016 election.

July 19, 2018

- At a security forum, Homeland Security Secretary Kirstjen Nielsen says, "I haven't seen any evidence that the attempt to interfere in our election infrastructure was to favor a particular political party. What we've seen on the foreign influence side is they were attempting to intervene and cause chaos on both sides."
- Sarah Huckabee Sanders announces that Trump plans to invite Vladimir Putin to Washington, D.C., in the fall. When told of the news at a security forum, Director of National Intelligence Dan Coats sarcastically remarks, "That's gonna be special."

From the Desk of Aldous J. Pennyfarthing
To: Donald Trump, Russian sock puppet

Dear Fucking Moron,

Psst, comrade. Maybe lie low for a while, okay? You've been made.

Putin will send out the Fat Signal if he *really* wants to talk to you. Or maybe you should just pick up that emergency red phone you've been using to order Jimmy John's.

And if he's traveling all the way to D.C., God knows what vital U.S. interest you'll cede to him this time. Maybe have the 1980 U.S. Olympic hockey team's gold medal rescinded? Order the ending changed on all extant VHS copies of *Rocky IV*?

Oh, I know! Alaska! We're not using that much of it anyway. And, to be fair, it's a lot closer to Russia than it is to most Americans —except for Alaskans, of course.

Anyway, if you're going to spill more closely held government secrets, maybe just tell him why your skin looks like a boiled squash rind. My leading theory? You accidentally got caught in one of Seth Brundle's telepods with a passed-out orangutan.

Love,
Pennyfarthing

◆ ◆ ◆

July 20, 2018

- Republican Sen. Jeff Flake harshly criticizes Trump's performance at the Helsinki summit, saying, "Well, we saw earlier this week in Helsinki what was a truly an Orwellian moment. What we saw earlier this week in Helsinki is what happens when you wage war on objective reality for nearly two solid years. Calling real things fake, and fake things, real."
- Trump claims President Obama was a "total patsy" for Russia.
- Several media outlets report that Michael Cohen recorded a conversation with Trump in which the two discussed a hush payment to a former Playboy model who allegedly had an affair with Trump.

◆ ◆ ◆

July 21, 2018

- Trump reacts to reports that his former lawyer Michael Cohen taped conversations between the two, tweeting, "Inconceivable that the government would break into a lawyer's office (early in the morning) - almost unheard of. Even more inconceivable that a lawyer would tape a client - totally unheard of & perhaps illegal. The good news is that your favorite President did nothing wrong!"

July 23, 2018

- Sarah Huckabee Sanders announces Trump is considering revoking the security clearances of some of his most vociferous critics, including former CIA Director John Brennan, former FBI Director James Comey, and former Director of National Intelligence James Clapper.
- Trump threatens Iranian President Hassan Rouhani with a fusillade of extra-scary capital letters, tweeting, "To Iranian President Rouhani: NEVER, EVER THREATEN THE UNITED STATES AGAIN OR YOU WILL SUFFER CONSEQUENCES THE LIKES OF WHICH FEW THROUGHOUT HISTORY HAVE EVER SUFFERED BEFORE. WE ARE NO LONGER A COUNTRY THAT WILL STAND FOR YOUR DEMENTED WORDS OF VIOLENCE & DEATH. BE CAUTIOUS!"

From the Desk of Aldous J. Pennyfarthing
To: Donald Trump, President Comic Sans

Dear Fucking Moron,

See, this is why you've accomplished more in your first two years than any president ever. CAPS LOCK!

That pussy John Adams never used caps lock. He was too afraid. And *way* too politically correct.

John Adams was our second president, by the way.

Oh, I'm sorry.

JOHN ADAMS WAS OUR SECOND PRESIDENT, BY THE WAY!!!!!!!!!!!

Wait, maybe I'm onto something here.

CLIMATE CHANGE IS REAL!!!!!!!

YOU DID NOT SAVE THE ECONOMY!!!!! OBAMA DID!!!!!!

YOUR FACE LOOKS LIKE A HAGGIS FUCKED A PRISON LAUNDRY HAMPER FULL OF EXPIRED GOUDA!!!!!!!! STOP SPRAY-TANNING, YOU FLUORESCENT FUCK!!!!!!!!!!

IMMIGRANTS CONTRIBUTE MORE TO OUR ECONOMY THAN THEY TAKE!!!!!

FOR GOD'S SAKE, STOP TELLING EVERYONE YOU WANT TO FUCK YOUR DAUGHTER!!!! I CAN'T EVEN BELIEVE I HAVE TO TELL YOU THIS!!!!!!

You know, that actually felt kind of good. I almost get it now.

Love,
Pennyfarthing

July 24, 2018

- The White House announces a $12 billion aid package for farmers who have been negatively affected by Trump's trade war.
- Trump tweets, "I'm very concerned that Russia will be fighting very hard to have an impact on the upcoming Election. Based on the fact that no President has

been tougher on Russia than me, they will be pushing very hard for the Democrats. They definitely don't want Trump!"

- During a speech at the Veterans of Foreign Wars national convention in Kansas City, Trump says, "What you're seeing and what you're reading is not what's happening."
- For at least the fifth time, Trump claims our Air Force has planes that are literally invisible: "This is an incredible plane. It's stealth—you can't see it!"

From the Desk of Aldous J. Pennyfarthing
To: Donald Trump, fanny pack full of moldy dicks

Dear Fucking Moron,

You've gotta spread the crazy out a bit more there, Wonder Woman. How am I supposed to keep up?

Let me help you out:

1. For the last time, invisible planes do not exist.
2. In consensus reality, what you see generally *is* what's happening. I mean, I have no idea what *you* see after you're done injecting Siberian reindeer urine into your eyeballs every morning, but the rest of us are pretty clear about what's really going on.
3. No one in Russia is trying to throw the election to Democrats, you fucking weirdo.
4. Glad to see you're trying to help out the farmers you've singlehandedly fucked over with your latest quaggy brain shart. That's really thoughtful of you. I'm sure they'll think back on you fondly as they're swinging listlessly from the hayloft.

I swear, every morning is like zipping open your Hello Kitty knapsack in order to find out which neighbor's severed head your mom stashed in there today. It's horrifying, but you're naturally curious. But this is just *way* too many heads at once. Pace yourself, man.

Love,
Pennyfarthing

◆ ◆ ◆

July 25, 2018

- Responding to critics of his protectionist trade policies, Trump tweets, "When you have people snipping at your heels during a negotiation, it will only take longer to make a deal, and the deal will never be as good as it could have been with unity. Negotiations are going really well, be cool. The end result will be worth it!"
- Reuters releases photos of Chinese workers making Trump's 2020 campaign flags.

◆ ◆ ◆

From the Desk of Aldous J. Pennyfarthing
To: Donald Trump, Minge the Merciless

Dear Fucking Moron,

The only thing more insane than you manufacturing campaign flags in China after all your shit-talking is ... well, I can't think of anything, actually. You might as well hire undocumented immigrants at your New Jersey golf club. Oh, wait, you do that, too. Never mind. How about you shove a 12-foot-wide framed Escher lithograph up your ass while you sing the Mexican national anthem in Portuguese while wearing a mesh thong and 14th-century pope's miter? And, hey, you've got two hands.

Might as well milk a rhinestone-bedazzled kangaroo tit while you're at it. Male or female. Doesn't matter. All fucking sense is out the fucking window at this point anyway.

And believe it or not, it gets worse.

Here's how Huffington Post described your latest adventure in mind-warping hypocrisy:

> "Photos released by Reuters on Wednesday show a Chinese factory making flags for President Donald Trump's 2020 re-election campaign.
>
> "Since March, Jiahao Flag Factory, located in Fuyang, Anhui province, has made approximately 90,000 of the flags for use at Trump campaign events, according to Reuters.
>
> "The flags reportedly cost about $1 apiece, a price that is likely to go up after Trump's tariffs on China kick in. The campaign's suppliers are likely trying to get these prices while they can, the factory manager told Reuters."

So you're trying to warehouse all this merch before *your own dumbass tariffs* make your grotesque exploitation of low-cost Chinese laborers cost-prohibitive?

That's a fun trick.

It's like how I've been stockpiling tequila and limes ahead of election night 2020 just in case I have to drink myself to death by morning for some reason.

Anyway, maybe it's not so bad. You could insist that they print "Made in China" in some exotic, arcane language your supporters have no hope of comprehending. You know, like English.

Love,
Pennyfarthing

July 26, 2018

- Michael Cohen claims that Trump knew in advance of the 2016 Trump Tower meeting with Russians who had offered dirt on Hillary Clinton.
- The court-imposed deadline to reunite families separated at the border under Trump's zero tolerance policy lapses, with hundreds of children still waiting to be reunited with their families.
- *The Wall Street Journal* reports that European Commission President Jean-Claude Juncker was forced to use flashcards to explain global trade to Trump.

From the Desk of Aldous J. Pennyfarthing
To: Donald Trump, global embarrassment

Dear Fucking Moron,

Okay, this was first reported in *The Wall Street Journal*, but Rupert Murdoch owns that paper now, and it has a paywall, and I'd rather spend a long weekend in a Tijuana hot tub with Steve Bannon watching him slowly dissolve like a tab of Alka-Seltzer than give that fucking Aus-hole more money, so here's Business Insider's synopsis instead:

> "The Journal's report says Juncker 'flipped through' more than a dozen cards, which had minimal information on them, and all focused on a single issue. These included the automotive trade, and regulatory standards for medicines, the report added, say-

ing that there were a maximum of three figures per card.

"'We knew this wasn't an academic seminar,' a senior EU official who was at the meeting told the Wall Street Journal. 'It had to be very simple.'"

Yeah, *very* simple. Like "blue is water, green is land" simple. Because for you, anything more complex than the McDonald's Dollar Menu might as well be supersymmetric string theory.

But, yeah, flashcards can be useful. For learning the difference between "b" and "d" when you're 4. Once you've mastered that, you're pretty much expected to read newspapers and, well, books. I know it's a tall order, but every president until now has been expected to do the same. Because they weren't goddamn children.

That said, I'm *so* glad the rest of the world is no longer laughing at us. Our long national nightmare finally is over.

Whew.

Love,
Pennyfarthing

◆ ◆ ◆

July 29, 2018

- Trump tweets, "I would be willing to 'shut down' government if the Democrats do not give us the votes for Border Security, which includes the Wall! Must get rid of Lottery, Catch & Release etc. and finally go to system of Immigration based on MERIT! We need great people coming into our Country!"

From the Desk of Aldous J. Pennyfarthing
To: Donald Trump, cosmic error

Dear Fucking Moron,

Just a few edits.

Lowercase "border," "security," "wall," "lottery," "catch," "release," "immigration," and "country."

Use ampersands sparingly. Think of them as healthy green vegetables.

There should be a comma before "etc."

You probably don't need to put MERIT in all caps. We get it. You already, quite unnecessarily, used an exclamation point.

You absolutely do not need to put "shut down" in quotation marks. For the life of me, I have no idea what you're trying to do with those. You're supposed to be our president, for fuck's sake. You look like a chef in a five-star restaurant using the citrus zester to lance a boil on your forehead.

Finally, we *do* need great people coming into our country, but we're about three generations too late on that one, Humpty Drumpfy.

Love,
Pennyfarthing

July 30, 2018

- Trump says he would be willing to meet with Iranian leaders without preconditions.
- NBA superstar Lebron James slams Trump in an interview, remarking, "We are in a position in America where this race thing has taken over. One, because I

believe our president is trying to divide us. He's kind of used sport to divide us, and that's something I can't relate to."

- In an interview with CNN, Trump's lawyer Rudy Giuliani says, "I don't even know if that's a crime, colluding about Russians."
- Speaking out in defense of voter ID laws, Trump says, "You know, if you go out and you want to buy groceries, you need a picture on a card; you need ID. You go out and you want to buy anything, you need ID and you need your picture."

From the Desk of Aldous J. Pennyfarthing
To: Donald Trump, golden toilet god

Dear Fucking Moron,

Dude, I have purchased Funyuns at Circle K at 4 a.m. while drunk, high, and with one penis Sharpied on my face and another drooping languidly from my bathrobe like a chloroformed kangaroo mouse*, and no one ever gave a flippin' fuck who I was.

They just take your money and instantly return to their humiliating porn-besotted lives. No one gives a shit.

What fucking world have you been living in?

Now we all know that you've never bought groceries, like, ever in your life.

Or is this simply another engorged fantasy about a police state where people carrying fennel bulbs and fresh pasta back to their tony brownstones are routinely asked to show their papers or be forced to eat curb?

Who ever thought that a guy who, through no fault of his own, was a millionaire by the age of 8 and flies around in a private plane with gold sinks could ever be so out of touch? It's crazy, isn't it?

By the way, in case you ever do visit a grocery store, they limit the samples you can eat to one or two. Unless you're a celebrity. Then you can just rip into Honey Nut Cheerios boxes like a shit-faced falcon. In fact, they expect it. Go nuts, man.

*Wait! I meant capybara! My cock is *huge*, gold-filigreed, and worth TEN BILLION DOLLARS!

Love,
Pennyfarthing

◆ ◆ ◆

August 1, 2018

- Trump tweets, "This is a terrible situation and Attorney General Jeff Sessions should stop this Rigged Witch Hunt right now, before it continues to stain our country any further."

◆ ◆ ◆

August 3, 2018

- An excerpt of former White House aide Omarosa Manigault Newman's book *Unhinged* is released. She writes, in part, "While watching the interview I realized that something real and serious was going on in Donald's brain. His mental decline could not be denied. Many didn't notice it as keenly as I did because I knew him way back when. They thought Trump was being Trump, off the cuff. But I knew something wasn't right."

From the Desk of Aldous J. Pennyfarthing
To: Donald Trump, bumbling clunge

Dear Fucking Moron,

Wait, do I really need to read a book to find out your "mental decline could not be denied"?

Anyway, for someone like you, a "mental decline" is kind of like skiing down a bunny hill to grab a beer in the lodge. It's not a huge loss. So you can no longer play Duck, Duck, Goose because you can't remember anything past the first "Duck." Big effing deal. It's not like you were working on a unified field theory and now all that progress is lost. It's more like that time I lost my grandma's recipe for Rice Krispies Treats.

And she "knew something wasn't right"? Hey, welcome to Planet Earth, Omarosa! Enjoy your stay. Don't eat any undercooked shrimp and try not to walk into any rotating airplane propellers. I'd read the book, but I'm already worried David Lynch is going to sue me for stealing his nightmares.

Love,
Pennyfarthing

August 5, 2018

- Trump tweets about his son Donald Jr.'s June 2016 Trump Tower meeting with a Russian attorney: "Fake News reporting, a complete fabrication, that I am concerned about the meeting my wonderful son, Donald, had in Trump Tower. This was a meeting to get information on an opponent, totally legal and done all the time in politics - and it went nowhere. I did not know about it!"

August 6, 2018

- Axios reports that Trump likes to record his own campaign rallies and watch them later "like an NFL coach reviewing game film."
- Trump tweets, "California wildfires are being magnified & made so much worse by the bad environmental laws which aren't allowing massive amounts of readily available water to be properly utilized. It is being diverted into the Pacific Ocean. Must also tree clear to stop fire from spreading!"

August 8, 2018

- Trump predicts a "giant Red Wave" will overtake the country during the midterm elections, tweeting, "RED WAVE!"

From the Desk of Aldous J. Pennyfarthing
To: Donald Trump, red scaremonger

Dear Fucking Moron,

I can always tell when it's you tweeting and not some lackey who's been irrevocably enervated by 19 straight months of dipshittery, KFC floor scraps, and Cronenberg-caliber unreality.

How?

Even an unpaid social media intern on his last day (of life, not on the job) would be *way* too embarrassed to ever tweet "RED WAVE!"

I mean, just because you do half your "work" from your toilet doesn't mean you have to live-tweet your urine stream, Captain Chlamydia.

And how exactly would you define a "red wave"? Because all the polls I see look bluer than Lindsey Graham's balls at a discount brothel.

Trust me. Not only will there *not* be a red wave, the red wave that will never be will fail to materialize because of *your* illiterate ass.

If you want "decent" Republicans to hold onto their seats, maybe don't defend Nazis and endorse pedophiles. It's a bad look, okay? Is it any wonder so many of them are recoiling from Your Heinous? I mean, you're basically the electoral equivalent of Gwyneth Paltrow's head at the end of *Se7en*.

So why do I think you're going to declare victory anyway after you get your ass kicked?

Well, because you're a delusional prick.

Occam's razor, man.

Love,
Pennyfarthing

August 9, 2018

- Mike Pence officially announces the administration's proposal for a new Space Force: "As President Trump has said, in his words, it is not enough to merely have an American presence in space — we must have American dominance in space. And so we will. Space is, in his words, a war-fighting domain just like land and air and sea."

- Trump tweets, "Space Force all the way!"

From the Desk of Aldous J. Pennyfarthing
To: Donald Trump, No. 1 Space Force cadet!

Dear Fucking Moron,

Space Force, Space Force, Space Force all the way!

Goooooo *Space Force!*

We've got Space Force, yes we do, we've got Space Force, how 'bout you!?

HERE I COME TO SAVE THE DAY!

Space Force all the *way!*

My nipples are titanium! And ready for ... SPACE FORCE!

I've been accepted to SPACE FORCE ACADEMY as a SPACE FORCE RECRUIT! And if my dick gets shot off by Klingons it will be preserved for all time in the frigid, inky abyss of *SPACE*.

Yaaaaaay, SPACE FORCE!

Love,
Pennyfarthing

August 10, 2018

- On Twitter, Trump tells NFL players protesting racial injustice by kneeling during the national anthem to "....Be happy, be cool! A football game, that fans are paying soooo much money to watch and enjoy, is no place to protest. Most of that money goes to the players anyway. Find another way to protest. Stand proudly for your National Anthem or be Suspended Without Pay!"

- China's vice agriculture minister, Han Jun, warns that U.S. producers could permanently lose their market share because of Trump's trade war: "Many countries have the willingness and they totally have the capacity to take over the market share the U.S. is enjoying in China. If other countries become reliable suppliers for China, it will be very difficult for the U.S. to regain the market."

August 11, 2018

- Asked about former White House aide Omarosa Manigault Newman, Trump responds, "Lowlife. She's a lowlife."
- One year after Charlottesville, Trump tweets out a limp-dicked call for unity.

From the Desk of Aldous J. Pennyfarthing
To: Donald Trump (who's looked at racism from both sides now)

Dear Fucking Moron,

Nice try, but no:

> "The riots in Charlottesville a year ago resulted in senseless death and division. We must come to-

gether as a nation. I condemn all types of racism and acts of violence. Peace to ALL Americans!"

All types of racism? Oh, whatever could that mean? That sounds a lot like "all lives matter" to me.

Here, let me fix your tweet for you, O Illustrious Tanned Dragon of the Cray-Cray-Cray:

> The ~~riots~~ **white supremacists** in Charlottesville a year ago ~~resulted in senseless death and division~~ **murdered an innocent woman who was fighting for racial justice and equality**. We must **condemn their acts** and come together as a nation. I condemn ~~all types of~~ racism and ~~acts of~~ **the senseless** violence **the alt-right caused last year. They have blood on their hands, and we cannot stand by while they continue to target people based solely on their race, ethnicity, sexual orientation, or religion**. Peace to ~~ALL Americans~~ **all victims of white supremacists and neo-Nazis!**

By the way, you're not fooling anyone with this next tweet, which came *15 fucking minutes* after your first nidorous geyser of minced baby shit:

> "I am proud to have fought for and secured the LOWEST African American and Hispanic unemployment rates in history. Now I'm pushing for prison reform to give people who have paid their debt to society a second chance. I will never stop fighting for ALL Americans!"

You're like the guy who shows up in the last 10 minutes of a painting party and eats all the pizza. Hint: Everyone hates that guy.

How exactly did you fight for these low unemployment numbers, Donnie Dipshits? Numbers that, only three years ago, you claimed were completely made up. What policies did you put in place to give people of color a boost?

Was it scrapping Obama's affirmative action guidelines?

Was it demoralizing people of color by attempting to delegitimize our nation's first African-American president, or by calling every African nation a "shithole country"?

Was it harassing productive, hardworking immigrants and DACA recipients who are just trying to build better lives and feed their families?

Was it phoning in your response to the devastation in Puerto Rico?

Or was it lying in bed at 10 a.m. licking cheese off Big Mac wrappers and coasting on Barack Obama's heroic efforts to reverse the ruinous policies of our last shithole president?

Take your time. I'll wait.

Love,
Pennyfarthing

◆ ◆ ◆

August 12, 2018

- A day after welcoming Bikers for Trump to the White House, Trump proposes a boycott of iconic U.S. manufacturer Harley-Davidson via Twitter: "Many @harleydavidson owners plan to boycott the company if manufacturing moves overseas. Great! Most other companies are coming in our direction, including Harley competitors. A really bad move! U.S. will soon have a level playing field, or better."

August 13, 2018

- Peter Strzok, who sent text messages critical of Trump during the 2016 presidential campaign, is fired.
- On Twitter, Trump insists that he never used the n-word.

From the Desk of Aldous J. Pennyfarthing
To: Donald Trump, apprentice human

Dear Fucking Moron,

Um, I know you're not very bright, but there's something *really* wrong with this tweet:

> ".@MarkBurnettTV called to say that there are NO TAPES of the Apprentice where I used such a terrible and disgusting word as attributed by Wacky and Deranged Omarosa. I don't have that word in my vocabulary, and never have. She made it up."

Hmm. By a bizarre cosmic coincidence, I *just* got a call from Queen Elizabeth assuring me there are NO ANSWERING MACHINE TAPES of me from the mid-'90s calling her a heinous limey slutbag.

Whew!

Anyway, we're all relieved to find out our pr*sident isn't a hateful bigot, as far as we know — except for all the times he is, of course.

Sorry, I have to cut this short. I have a few calls to make. Gotta check with Walmart to see if I've been caught on any security tapes having boisterous howler monkey sex with Marcus Bachmann on a giant dragon-hoard pile of Cinnamon Toast Crunch.

Not that there's *any* way a tape like that could exist, but you can never be too careful about these things.

Love,
Pennyfarthing

August 14, 2018

- Magician Penn Jillette claims Mark Burnett is sitting on politically damaging tapes of Trump making offensive remarks during the shooting of *Celebrity Apprentice*. "I was in the room," he says.
- Referring to Omarosa Manigault Newman, Trump tweets, "When you give a crazed, crying lowlife a break, and give her a job at the White House, I guess it just didn't work out. Good work by General Kelly for quickly firing that dog!"

August 15, 2018

- Trump revokes former CIA Director John Brennan's security clearance.

August 16, 2018

- In a series of editorials, more than 300 newspapers across the country rebuke Trump for his broad attacks on the press.

August 17, 2018

- Trump tweets that he canceled his Washington military parade over cost concerns: "The local politicians who run Washington, D.C. (poorly) know a windfall when they see it. When asked to give us a price for holding a great celebratory military parade, they wanted a number so ridiculously high that I cancelled it. Never let someone hold you up! I will instead... ....attend the big parade already scheduled at Andrews Air Force Base on a different date, & go to the Paris parade, celebrating the end of the War, on November 11th. Maybe we will do something next year in D.C. when the cost comes WAY DOWN. Now we can buy some more jet fighters!"

From the Desk of Aldous J. Pennyfarthing
To: Donald Trump, shart of the deal

Dear Fucking Moron,

1. What the fuck were you planning on celebrating? Day One of our glorious new banana republic?
2. Was the cost high because they'd have to replace all the roads that were going to be ripped to shreds by tanks?
3. If Andrews Air Force Base already has a parade, why didn't you just plan on attending that one?
4. This parade was going to cost as much as several jets and yet you wanted to hold it anyway ... instead of, I don't know, buying more jets?
5. Parades are tedious as shit, dude. I haven't watched the Macy's Thanksgiving Day Parade in, like, 30 years, even though for a significant stretch of that

time there was a real chance that a float full of My Little Ponies would crash into Matt Lauer.

And this is a brilliant negotiating tactic, by the way. Refuse to put on a parade that no one in Washington except you actually wants to see ... *until the price comes down!* Oh, my. They're going to crack any second now. I can feel it. Next year they'll come begging, offering to give you your parade for a lot less because THE MASTER DEALMAKER HAS SPOKEN! ALL WILL COWER IN YOUR PRESENCE ... because ... REASONS!

MAGA, baby!

#Winning

Love,
Pennyfarthing

◆ ◆ ◆

August 18, 2018

- Trump attempts to defend his revocation of John Brennan's security clearance: "Has anyone looked at the mistakes that John Brennan made while serving as CIA Director?" he tweets. "He will go down as easily the WORST in history & since getting out, he has become nothing less than a loudmouth, partisan, political hack who cannot be trusted with the secrets to our country!"
- Apparently responding to some social media companies' efforts to stifle conspiracy theorist Alex Jones, Trump tweets, "Social Media is totally discriminating against Republican/Conservative voices. Speaking loudly and clearly for the Trump Administration, we won't let that happen. They are closing down the opinions of many people on the RIGHT, while at the same time doing nothing to others."

- *The New York Times* reports that White House Counsel Don McGahn has been cooperating with Robert Mueller. Trump later tweets, "The failing @nytimes wrote a Fake piece today implying that because White House Councel [sic] Don McGahn was giving hours of testimony to the Special Councel [sic], he must be a John Dean type 'RAT.' But I allowed him and all others to testify - I didn't have to. I have nothing to hide……"
- In an interview with *Meet the Press*, Rudy Giuliani says, "Truth isn't truth."

August 20, 2018

- After watching former intelligence official Phillip Mudd become agitated during a CNN interview, Trump hints that he might revoke his security clearance, tweeting, "Mudd is in no mental condition to have such a Clearance."
- Trump congratulates border patrol agent Adrian Anzaldua for discovering 78 undocumented immigrants in a trailer in Texas and marvels that he "speaks perfect English."

From the Desk of Aldous J. Pennyfarthing
To: Donald Trump, bellend of the world as we know it

Dear Fucking Moron,

Okay, so remember this?

> "Come here. You're not nervous, right? Speaks perfect English. Come here, I want to ask you about

that, 78 lives. You saved 78 people."

He speaks perfect English, huh? Well, someone on that stage has to.

I bet you're *just* as surprised he didn't ride up to the dais on a burro while playing "La Cucaracha" on a Mariachi guitar.

My God, even when you're trying to be *nice* you're irretrievably racist. Yes, many, many nonwhite people are extremely good at their jobs. And many white people are incompetent buffoons. Just look at the difference between our previous president and our current one. It's a small sample size but, oh, what a sample!

I guess this is one of those fabled "good people" with brown skin you always assumed were as rare as glitter-farting unicorns.

Jesus Christ, you can't even do a simple photo op without sharting your fucking charro pants.

Love,
Pennyfarthing

August 21, 2018

- Former Trump campaign chair Paul Manafort is convicted on eight felony counts. Trump responds by saying, "It doesn't involve me, but I still feel it is a very sad thing that happened. This has nothing to do with Russian collusion."
- Michael Cohen pleads guilty to campaign finance violations in connection with hush money payments he arranged, allegedly on Trump's behalf, to porn star Stormy Daniels.

August 22, 2018

- Trump tweets, "If anyone is looking for a good lawyer, I would strongly suggest that you don't retain the services of Michael Cohen!" Cohen worked for Trump for more than 10 years.
- *The Wall Street Journal* reports that *National Enquirer* publisher and Trump pal David Pecker is cooperating with federal prosecutors in the Trump-Russia probe.

August 23, 2018

- When asked during a *Fox & Friends* interview what grade he'd give himself for his performance as president, Trump responds, "I give myself an A+."

♦ ♦ ♦

From the Desk of Aldous J. Pennyfarthing
To: Donald Trump, extreme left-hand side of the bell curve

Dear Fucking Moron,

Oh, for fuck's sake, just stop it, you piss-bloated screech owl.

Needless to say, this is 31 flavors of crazy:

> "I give myself an A+. I don't think any president has ever done what I've done in this short ... we haven't even been two years."
>
> ...
>
> "If I ever got impeached, I think the market would

crash, I think everybody would be very poor. You would see numbers that you wouldn't believe."

You know, I wouldn't necessarily mind living a quiet, simple life in a rustic New England sewer with Pennywise the creepy homicidal clown. Pennywise 'n' Pennyfarthing, BFFs.

If it means you're no longer president? Sure. Bring it on. How bad can cockroach parmigiana be?

What's more, I'd be happy to cash in my 401(k) and sell 12 pints of plasma to raise the money for your bon voyage parade. Not *my* plasma, of course. That would be nuts. But I'm sure I could find some *somewhere*.

Anything — *anything* — to get rid of your turgid blue-ribbon butternut squash of a head.

But ...

None of that would happen, because you don't control the economy, Witchiepoo.

So the same S&P 500 index that nearly *tripled* under Obama would suddenly take a nosedive because you're groping cleavage in a different ZIP code? Nope.

You inherited a thriving economy and a robust stock market. Give someone else credit for *something* for once.

Oh, and job growth has actually *slowed* since you took over. Try tweeting *that* out to your horde of flying monkeys, Maleficent.

Love,
Pennyfarthing

August 24, 2018

- Trump cancels Secretary of State Mike Pompeo's visit

to North Korea, tweeting, "I have asked Secretary of State Mike Pompeo not to go to North Korea, at this time, because I feel we are not making sufficient progress with respect to the denuclearisation of the Korean Peninsula."

- *The Wall Street Journal* reports that Trump Organization CFO Allen Weisselberg is cooperating with federal prosecutors.

August 26, 2018

- Trump reportedly nixes a White House statement praising John McCain in the wake of the senator's death, instead tweeting condolences to McCain's family.

August 27, 2018

- After prematurely raising the American flag, the White House re-lowers it to half-staff following Sen. John McCain's death. *The Wall Street Journal* later reports that Trump had refused to lower the flag because he thought the media coverage of McCain's passing was "over-the-top and more befitting a president."

August 28, 2018

- On Twitter, Trump claims Google is rigging its search results: "Google search results for 'Trump News' shows only the viewing/reporting of Fake News Media. In other words, they have it RIGGED, for me

& others, so that almost all stories & news is BAD. ... This is a very serious situation-will be addressed!"

- *The Washington Post* reports that Trump told Japanese Prime Minister Shinzo Abe, during a tense meeting over trade, "I remember Pearl Harbor."

◆ ◆ ◆

August 29, 2018

- *Washington Post* reporter David Fahrenthold notes that another Trump brand has taken a dirt nap: ".@realDonaldTrump once had 19 companies paying him to use his name on their products. By this yr, just 2 were left. Now, it might be 1. Panamanian company HomeStudio S.A., which sold Trump-branded bed linens in Latin America, has shut website and stopped answering the phone."
- Politico reports that Trump can't stand Attorney General Jeff Sessions' Southern accent.

◆ ◆ ◆

From the Desk of Aldous J. Pennyfarthing
To: Donald Trump, hillbilly heroine

Dear Fucking Moron,

Hey, did you happen to see this Politico article? It's crazy, man. Here's an excerpt:

> "Seized by paroxysms of anger, Trump has intermittently pushed to fire his attorney general since March 2017, when Sessions announced his recusal from the Russia investigation. If Sessions' recusal was his original sin, Trump has come to resent him for other reasons, griping to aides and lawmakers

that the attorney general doesn't have the Ivy League pedigree the president prefers, that he can't stand his Southern accent and that Sessions isn't a capable defender of the president on television — in part because he 'talks like he has marbles in his mouth,' the president has told aides."

Well, you talk like you have marbles in your head, so ...

Poor Jeff Sessions. The only senator who was dumb enough to support you from the beginning, and now he's got all the dignity of a TGI Fridays urinal cake.

But, whoa! You're going to criticize someone else's accent? Dude, you sound like a cross between Tony Danza, a crashing helicopter, and a syphilitic chicken.

And, hey, Southerners are pretty much your base. Have you seen your electoral map? Wait, who the fuck am I talking to? You stare at that thing so much you might as well have it tattooed on Ivanka's ass ... you know, so you can free up eight hours or so of your workweek.

Glad to see you value loyalty so highly. That is, others' loyalty toward you. I have a feeling you'd give Donald Jr. up to Bob Mueller for a Bed Bath & Beyond coupon.

Love,
Pennyfarthing

August 30, 2018

- Trump announces that he'll cancel a pay raise for federal workers that was due to take effect in January 2019.
- Trump says during a Bloomberg News interview that Jeff Sessions' job is safe until after the midterm elec-

tions.

◆ ◆ ◆

August 31, 2018

- At a campaign rally in Indiana, Trump says, "All I can say is our Justice Department and our FBI, at the top of each because inside they have incredible people, our Justice Department and our FBI have to start doing their job and doing it right. What's happening is a disgrace and at some point — I wanted to stay out — but at some point if it doesn't straighten out properly ... I will get involved." He also claims, "We're so far ahead of schedule" in making America great again.
- Trump's disapproval rating hits a new high of 60 percent in the ABC/*Washington Post* poll. Fifty-three percent of respondents say they disapprove of him "strongly."
- Trump tweets, "I will be doing a major rally for Senator Ted Cruz in October. I'm picking the biggest stadium in Texas we can find. As you know, Ted has my complete and total Endorsement. His opponent is a disaster for Texas - weak on Second Amendment, Crime, Borders, Military, and Vets!"

From the Desk of Aldous J. Pennyfarthing
To: Donald Trump, Lyin' Dread

Dear Fucking Moron,

So you eventually held your big Ted Cruz rally at Houston's Toyota Center, which has a seating capacity of 18,300. The biggest venue in Texas is Texas A&M University's Kyle Field, which holds 102,733. So you were only off by 84,433 people. Not bad!

Still, I loved your tweet about your Ted Cruz rally. So bold.

I also loved this one:

> "How can Ted Cruz be an Evangelical Christian when he lies so much and is so dishonest?"

Oh, and then there's this thing Cruz said about *you*:

> "This man is a pathological liar. He doesn't know the difference between truth and lies. In a pattern that is straight out of a psychology textbook, he accuses everyone of lying."

Frankly, I think you were both right — which is kind of like all the planets aligning at the precise moment Bill O'Reilly accepts a Grammy for the vinyl release of his falafel sex tapes.

Interesting, though, that Cruz has to desperately fend off a challenge from a Democrat in Texas, of all places. Normally all a Republican has to do to win a Texas Senate race is ensure that his ads aren't just raw blooper reel footage from his latest colonoscopy video.

Anyway, kudos on your hearty endorsement of Ted Cruz, who is almost certainly not a serial killer.

Though his dad *may* have been part of a conspiracy to kill JFK, according to some idiot who should probably be locked up, frankly.

Love,
Pennyfarthing

September 1, 2018

- Citing presidential privilege, the Trump administration withholds more than 100,000 pages of records

from Brett Kavanaugh's work with the Bush administration.

- Amid trade negotiations, Trump tweets, "I love Canada, but they've taken advantage of our Country for
many years!"
- At her father's memorial service, Meghan McCain
says, "The America of John McCain has no need to
be made great again because America was always
great." Later that day, Trump tweets, "MAKE AMER-
ICA GREAT AGAIN!"

From the Desk of Aldous J. Pennyfarthing
To: Donald Trump, coward of the country (aka Kenny Rogers
chicken)

Dear Fucking Moron,

So remember that time you mocked that disabled reporter
and then spent the next three years claiming you hadn't, even
though everyone in the country saw you do it?

Oh, those were the days — back when I still thought things, you
know, mattered. Before my soft, earnest heart turned to obsid-
ian and my ineluctably shrinking sphincter gradually withered
from the size of a tweaking lemur's balled-up fist to a Planck-
length gravitational singularity that could warp titanium rebar
from 100 light-years away.

So, yeah, mocking the disabled reporter over his disability was,
like, your "I love Brian Piccolo" moment. We'll remember it forever as the capstone of a life sincerely and faithfully devoted to
flopping around like a morbidly obese sea otter in hog shit.

Because every time I think you've reached a nadir, it just gets so,
so, *so* much worse.

Case in point:

Today, at John McCain's *funeral*, for fuck's sake, his daughter Meghan said this during her eulogy for her father:

> "The America of John McCain is generous and welcoming and bold. She is resourceful and confident and secure. She meets her responsibilities. She speaks quietly because she is strong. America does not boast because she has no need. The America of John McCain has no need to be made great again because America was always great."

And your Churchillian response (via Twitter, of course) to this woman who was suffering through profound grief and one of the most fraught moments of her young life?

"MAKE AMERICA GREAT AGAIN!"

You might recognize that catchphrase. It's on millions of hats hiding millions of lobotomy scars on millions of spongy heads across our great nation.

So, basically, you're an 8-year-old ... in a 72-year-old manatee's body.

Also, fuck you sideways, you flaccid wasp dick.

Seriously.

Love,
Pennyfarthing

◆ ◆ ◆

September 3, 2018

- On Twitter, Trump accuses Jeff Sessions of endangering the reelection of two GOP congressmen: "Two long running, Obama era, investigations of two very popular Republican Congressmen were brought to a well publicized charge, just ahead of the Mid-Terms, by the Jeff Sessions Justice Department. Two easy wins now in doubt because there is not enough time. Good job Jeff...."

- Rudy Giuliani tells *The New Yorker* that the Trump administration will likely attempt to prevent Robert Mueller's final report from being released to the public.

◆ ◆ ◆

September 4, 2018

- Excerpts from Bob Woodward's book *Fear* are released, and it ain't good. Among the revelations: Trump economic adviser Gary Cohn stole a letter off Trump's desk to prevent the pr*sident from nixing a South Korean trade deal. Cohn assumed, correctly, that Trump would simply forget about the letter.

◆ ◆ ◆

From the Desk of Aldous J. Pennyfarthing
To: Donald Trump, parlous arsegoblin

Dear Fucking Moron,

Don't worry. Nobody reads Bob Woodward. Has anyone even heard of this guy? He's FAKE NEWS! Or, you know, whatever the two-time Pulitzer Prize-winning version of that *fascista* slogan would be.

So your advisers were stealing shit off your desk so you didn't make ridiculous unforced errors? Sounds about right. Can they use the parental controls on your cable box to block Fox News, too? Might as well cut the bullshit off at the source. If they can't legally chloroform you and stick you in an airlock on the International Space Station for the next two years, at the *very* least they can make you stop mind-melding with Brian Kilmeade.

I also like this quote from John Kelly: "It's pointless to try to convince him of anything. He's gone off the rails. We're in Crazytown."

Personally, I think we passed Crazytown about 12 exits back, right before we stopped to pee in Narnia. Now we're in Willy Wonka's chocolate factory, and you're Augustus Gloop about two seconds away from getting sucked up the chocolate-river tube.

Call me crazy, but if someone had written an entire book about how insane and unfit I am for *my* job, I might spend an afternoon in quiet reflection instead of, I don't know, a hot fudge coma.

Love,
Pennyfarthing

◆ ◆ ◆

September 5, 2018

- Trump tweets, "Almost everyone agrees that my Administration has done more in less than two years than any other Administration in the history of our Country. I'm tough as hell on people & if I weren't, nothing would get done. Also, I question everybody & everything-which is why I got elected!"
- *The New York Times* publishes an editorial from a senior White House official who claims he or she is part of the Trump "resistance," which is actively working to undermine the pr*sident. Trump later tweets, "TREASON?"

◆ ◆ ◆

From the Desk of Aldous J. Pennyfarthing
To: Donald Trump, dangerously incompetent tub of adipose

Dear Fucking Moron,

OH. MY. GOD.

This editorial. Yikes!

I'll bet your head is overheating and making knocking noises like an old Victorian radiator right around now.

Who do you think wrote it? Don't be paranoid, but I think it's Pence. That guy wants to be president *so*, so bad. And I'm sure he will be after he finds a way to 86 your amoral shit midden of a presidency. I'm already keying my masturbation history into an Excel file for my applications to the nation's finest Christian re-education camps and, ironically, it's giving me carpal tunnel.

So which are your favorite parts? I mean, the whole thing is basically an admission that having you as president feels like smuggling a colony of bullet ants up your ass in a wax Dixie cup.

But this part is probably my favorite:

> "Given the instability many witnessed, there were early whispers within the cabinet of invoking the 25th Amendment, which would start a complex process for removing the president. But no one wanted to precipitate a constitutional crisis. So we will do what we can to steer the administration in the right direction until — one way or another — it's over.

> "The bigger concern is not what Mr. Trump has done to the presidency but rather what we as a nation have allowed him to do to us. We have sunk low with him and allowed our discourse to be stripped of civility."

Guh.

That's gotta sting, huh?

My ex-coworkers used to talk about me behind my back because I ate the same thing for lunch every day and used too much Sriracha. I can't imagine how I'd have felt if they'd anonymously tacked a letter to the break room bulletin board saying I was a pulp-brained lunatic who was destroying the company.

I probably would have been pretty mad, actually.

You should just fire everyone. Start over. Go down to Shoney's and make the night-shift line cooks your cabinet. What the fuck difference does it make at this point, honestly?

Love,
Pennyfarthing

September 6, 2018

- Axios reports that Trump once carried a list of people he suspected to be leakers. A source told the website, "He would basically be like, 'We've gotta get rid of them. The snakes are everywhere but we're getting rid of them.'"

◆ ◆ ◆

September 7, 2018

- Trump blasts critics of Supreme Court nominee Brett Kavanaugh, saying, "It's embarrassing to watch those people make fools of themselves as they scream and shout at this great gentleman."

- Trump says he wants Attorney General Jeff Sessions to launch an investigation into who said mean things about him in a recent anonymous *New York Times* editorial.

September 9, 2018

- Trump again attacks the NFL via Twitter: "Wow, NFL first game ratings are way down over an already really bad last year comparison. Viewership declined 13%, the lowest in over a decade. If the players stood proudly for our Flag and Anthem, and it is all shown on broadcast, maybe ratings could come back? Otherwise worse!"

September 10, 2018

- Trump tweets, "'President Trump would need a magic wand to get to 4% GDP,' stated President Obama. I guess I have a magic wand, 4.2%, and we will do MUCH better than this! We have just begun." In reality, the country reported GDPs in excess of 4.2 percent three times under Obama, including growth of 4.9 percent and 5.1 percent in two quarters of 2014. Obama was talking about yearly GDP growth, and Trump has yet to achieve 3 percent growth in a single year, and likely never will. Because, again, he's a moron.
- An excerpt from Bob Woodward's *Fear* reveals that former top economic adviser Gary Cohn came away from his first meeting with Trump astounded by how stupid he was.

◆ ◆ ◆

From the Desk of Aldous J. Pennyfarthing
To: Donald Trump, kettle of codswallop

Dear Fucking Moron,

Personally, I'm astounded that anyone could be astounded about how astoundingly stupid you are, but apparently Gary Cohn once had enough faith in you to think you wouldn't be the presidential equivalent of a flock of pelicans with convulsive diarrhea.

From Bob Woodward's *Fear* (I know, I know; fake news):

> "Next, Cohn repeated what everyone was saying: Interest rates were going to go up over the foreseeable future.
>
> "I agree, Trump said. 'We should just go borrow a lot of money right now, hold it, and then sell it and make money.'
>
> "Cohn was astounded at Trump's lack of basic understanding. He tried to explain. If you as the federal government borrow money through issuing bonds, you are increasing the U.S. deficit.
>
> "What do you mean? Trump asked. Just run the presses—print money.
>
> "You don't get to do it that way, Cohn said. We have huge deficits and they matter."

And ... scene.

Wait, didn't you promise to eliminate the entire national debt in eight years? Ah ... never mind. You just say random things for shits and giggles. No one really cares.

And, to be fair, there's a *lot* you don't understand. You can throw government debt on the pile with climate science, foreign policy, vaccines, the economy as a whole, consensus reality, and how to wear a tie without looking like a Depression-era street urchin who stole a suit off a frozen hobo.

Don't worry. We're laughing with you, not at you. You're a very, very smart boy. Everyone says so. No, really.

Love,
Pennyfarthing

◆ ◆ ◆

September 12, 2018

- As Hurricane Florence approaches the Southeast, Trump tweets, "We got A Pluses for our recent hurricane work in Texas and Florida (and did an unappreciated great job in Puerto Rico, even though an inaccessible island with very poor electricity and a totally incompetent Mayor of San Juan). We are ready for the big one that is coming!"

◆ ◆ ◆

September 13, 2018

- After J.P. Morgan Chase CEO Jamie Dimon says he could defeat Trump in an election, Trump tweets, "The problem with banker Jamie Dimon running for President is that he doesn't have the aptitude or 'smarts' & is a poor public speaker & nervous mess - otherwise he is wonderful. I've made a lot of bankers, and others, look much smarter than they are with my great economic policy!"

- In a report on the government's preparations for Hurricane Florence, *The Washington Post* writes, "Officials have brought large, colored charts and graphs into the Oval Office to illustrate Florence's dangerous path for Trump, who is a visual learner."
- In the wake of a George Washington University study that pegged the Puerto Rico death toll from Hurricane Maria at 2,975, Trump tweets, "3000 people did not die in the two hurricanes that hit Puerto Rico. When I left the Island, AFTER the storm had hit, they had anywhere from 6 to 18 deaths. As time went by it did not go up by much. Then, a long time later, they started to report really large numbers, like 3000... This was done by the Democrats in order to make me look as bad as possible when I was successfully raising Billions of Dollars to help rebuild Puerto Rico. If a person died for any reason, like old age, just add them onto the list. Bad politics. I love Puerto Rico!"

From the Desk of Aldous J. Pennyfarthing
To: Donald Trump, solipsistic shitnubbin

Dear Fucking Moron,

Hey, I know we don't agree on a lot — because I'm a normal human and you're an Igloo cooler full of antibiotic-resistant clown syphilis — but I know what you mean about Puerto Rico, man.

How dare anyone "study" those "deaths"? What calumny! Didn't they *once* stop to consider how this would make *you* feel? Obviously not.

Anyway, I had a very similar experience once.

My babysitter from when I was 4 was in the hospital, and she was breathing just fine with the help of three machines, a Korean War surplus aspirator, and twice-daily adrenaline shots, and then two days later I read in the paper that she's dead.

Bullshit!

I'd just *seen* her, man. FAKE OBIT!

Yeah, maybe I picked a bad time to tell her the pope had been shot, but what are you gonna do? It was an above-the-fold Page 1 story. I'd already read her that day's Marmaduke and she started ripping the IVs out of her arm like diseased cornstalks. I don't really blame her, but still.

Stay strong, bud. Your response to Hurricane Maria was as good as anyone could expect given that Puerto Rico is an island surrounded by water chock-full of sharks and jellyfish and plastic soda can rings and stuff. And saltwater, too. Did you ever get that shit in your eyes? Ugh.

How dare anyone say you don't care about brown people? You've seen, like, eight episodes of *Chico and the Man*.

What the fuck do they even want?

Island.

Surrounded by water.

What exactly aren't they getting?

Sheesh.

Love,
Pennyfarthing

❖ ❖ ❖

September 16, 2018

• Trump tweets, "While my (our) poll numbers are

good, with the Economy being the best ever, if it weren't for the Rigged Russian Witch Hunt, they would be 25 points higher! Highly conflicted Bob Mueller & the 17 Angry Democrats are using this Phony issue to hurt us in the Midterms. No Collusion!"

September 17, 2018

- Trump cuts the number of refugees allowed into the U.S. in 2019 to 30,000.
- Trump claims his trade war is going swimmingly, tweeting, "Tariffs have put the U.S. in a very strong bargaining position, with Billions of Dollars, and Jobs, flowing into our Country - and yet cost increases have thus far been almost unnoticeable. If countries will not make fair deals with us, they will be 'Tariffed!'"
- Christine Blasey Ford is revealed as the woman who has accused Brett Kavanaugh of sexual assault. Trump says he won't withdraw Kavanaugh's nomination.

September 18, 2018

- An excerpt of Stormy Daniels' book *Full Disclosure* is released. Of Trump's stimulus package she writes, "He knows he has an unusual penis. It has a huge mushroom head. Like a toadstool. ... I lay there, annoyed that I was getting fucked by a guy with Yeti pubes and a dick like the mushroom character in Mario Kart. ... It may have been the least impressive sex I'd ever had, but clearly, he didn't share that opinion."
- In a prepared video, Trump says Hurricane Florence is "one of the wettest we've ever seen from the stand-

point of water."

◆ ◆ ◆

From the Desk of Aldous J. Pennyfarthing
To: Donald Trump, Agua Man

Dear Fucking Moron,

You know, I was a little concerned that Hurricane Florence had suctioned up 18 trillion gallons of flop sweat while passing over one of your Alabama rallies, but thank God you have extraordinary access to NOAA data and can set us straight.

It's actually just *water*. Go figure.

In fact, it's "one of the wettest we've ever seen from the standpoint of ..."

Ha ha ha ha ha! Come on! You didn't think I'd pass up the chance to talk about your mushroom dick, did you?

Dude!

Ordinarily this whole thing would tickle my schadenfreude bone to no end, but it's totally put me off my two favorite pastimes: playing Mario Kart and crocheting ornate Victorian tea cozies out of molted Cascade Mountain Range yeti pubes. Oh, and masturbation. That's completely off the table now, too, of course. Congratulations. You accomplished in three seconds what 11 years of Catholic schooling never could.

So, once again, fuck you, you fungal fucknugget.

Anyway, maybe you can devise some kind of comb-over so the yeti pubes camouflage the mushroom penis. I'm thinking it would take one, maybe two pubes at most. You do know what I mean when I say "comb-over," right?

So, yeah, the takeaway from all this is that our pr*sident's groin is essentially a random square yard of Pacific Northwest forest floor. That's refreshing.

And now I fear I'm focusing far too much attention on the yeti pubes and completely neglecting the mushroom penis — which, technically, is Melania's job. Though I'm happy to do it, too, of course.

Love,
Pennyfarthing

◆ ◆ ◆

September 19, 2018

- In a Hill.TV interview, Trump once again attacks Jeff Sessions, saying, "I don't have an attorney general."
- Yahoo! News reports that the Department of Health and Human Services is diverting $80 million from vital programs — including Head Start, the National Cancer Institute, the Ryan White HIV/AIDS program, and programs focused on women's shelters, substance abuse, and maternal health — to pay for housing for detained immigrant children.

◆ ◆ ◆

September 21, 2018

- Multiply accused alleged sexual assaulter Donald Trump attacks Brett Kavanaugh accuser Christine Blasey Ford, tweeting, "I have no doubt that, if the attack on Dr. Ford was as bad as she says, charges would have been immediately filed with local Law Enforcement Authorities by either her or her loving parents. I ask that she bring those filings forward so that we can learn date, time, and place!"

September 23, 2018

- *The New Yorker* reports that another woman, Deborah Ramirez, has made a sexual assault allegation against Brett Kavanaugh.

September 24, 2018

- Trump once again defends Brett Kavanaugh, remarking, "There's a chance that this could be one of the single most unfair, unjust things to happen to a candidate for anything."

From the Desk of Aldous J. Pennyfarthing
To: Donald Trump, whiner-in-chief

Dear Fucking Moron,

I know you have an extremely tenuous grasp of human history, but what the fuck is this?

> "There's a chance that this could be one of the single most unfair, unjust things to happen to a candidate for anything."

Uh, Robert F. Kennedy was *fucking assassinated* while campaigning for president, you recidivous festoon of holiday elf turds. You are so fucking stupid, your brain probably looks like one of those mangled balls of suet my dad used to hang outside in winter for the nuthatches.

Also, gee, I don't know. The Comey letter? Remember that fun little October surprise?

Also, Merrick Garland kind of got screwed, don't you think?

Or is it possible you only have sympathy for multiply accused (alleged) sexual offenders because you've been accused of sexual assault numerous times, too, and you know how much it hurts deep down inside when people find out you're a giant perv lagoon.

So, of course, you're taking the side of the abusive creep again. Very predictable. How many times is this now?

Too many to count without throwing up, I know that much.

Love,
Pennyfarthing

September 25, 2018

- Members of the UN General Assembly openly laugh at Trump after he says, "In less than two years my administration has accomplished more than almost any administration in the history of our country."

From the Desk of Aldous J. Pennyfarthing
To: Donald Trump, coattails jockey

Dear Fucking Moron,

Let's see, President Obama likely averted a second Great Depression and passed comprehensive health care reform in his first two years.

You defended Nazis, endorsed a pedophile, undermined NATO, shivved our allies, took the word of a brutal dictator over our own intelligence agencies, signed a tax reform bill that disproportionately benefited the wealthy, repeatedly lied to your poor and middle-class supporters about who actually benefited from it, lied about the size of your inauguration crowd, threw paper towels at some Puerto Ricans, threw the health insurance exchanges into chaos by sabotaging Obamacare every chance you got, banned brave transgender soldiers from serving in our military, started a ruinous trade war, repeatedly undermined trust in the FBI and the rule of law, picked a fight with the Australian prime minister over nothing, helped steal a Supreme Court seat, authorized a commando raid in Yemen that led to disaster, fired your secretary of state via Twitter, nominated a secretary of education who knew virtually nothing about educating, walked around every day with an unsecured cellphone, repeatedly harangued your own attorney general, accused Obama of wiretapping your secret villain's lair, fired the FBI director for no good reason, gave away classified secrets to the Russian ambassador, lost track of an aircraft carrier, took the side of a man who murdered a U.S. resident, lied about a meeting with Russians in Trump Tower, and much, much, *much* more.

So, yeah, that's *technically* more things.

Also, Thomas Jefferson was a lightweight. Totally overrated. Why the fuck would he purchase Louisiana? That's one of our *states!* Worst deal in history — and you know deals, believe me.

Yes, when it comes to presidenting, everyone else is playing checkers, and you have the cellophane from the Candyland box wrapped around your head and are starting to turn blue.

You win.

At being a global laughingstock.

Congrats.

Love,
Pennyfarthing

September 27, 2018

- Christine Blasey Ford and Brett Kavanaugh testify separately at a Senate Judiciary Committee hearing concerning Ford's sexual assault allegations against Kavanaugh.

September 29, 2018

- At a West Virginia rally, Trump says he and Kim Jong Un "fell in love." "I was really tough and so was he, and we went back and forth. And then we fell in love, okay? No, really, he wrote me beautiful letters, and they're great letters. We fell in love."

September 30, 2018

- Despite being given a strict time limit and facing other severe restrictions, the FBI, according to Trump, has "free rein" to investigate sexual assault allegations against Brett Kavanaugh. "They're going to do whatever they have to do, whatever it is they do. They'll be doing things that we have never even thought of."

October 1, 2018

- During a press conference announcing a new U.S.-

Mexico-Canada trade agreement, Trump refers to critics of his tariffs as "babies."

- Taking questions from reporters, Trump insults ABC's senior White House correspondent, Cecilia Vega, saying, "That's okay. I know you're not thinking. You never do."

October 2, 2018

- *The New York Times* publishes a 15,000-word story revealing that Donald Trump and his family dodged tens of millions of dollars in taxes through a series of legally dubious methods.
- At a rally in Mississippi, Trump mocks Brett Kavanaugh accuser Christine Blasey Ford.

◆ ◆ ◆

From the Desk of Aldous J. Pennyfarthing
To: Donald Trump, dishonorable discharge

Dear Fucking Moron,

My friends and I have a pool in which we try to predict what execrable, incomprehensibly subhuman thing you're going to do next.

Today, I had "walk on-stage in a custom-tailored 1930s mob suit made of freshly harvested baby seal viscera and skull-fuck a dying giant panda with a flaming original copy of the Constitution up your ass while Ted Nugent stands next to you singing 'God Bless America' and masturbating on a Theravada Buddhist nun stapled ass-to-mouth to an elderly World War II veteran in a gimp suit," but it turns out I *really* undershot.

So what the fuck were you thinking here, you pestilential pint of curdled Fabio spooge?

From *The Washington Post*:

> "Trump, in a riff that has been dreaded by White House and Senate aides, attacked the story of Christine Blasey Ford at length — drawing laughs from the crowd. The remarks were his strongest attacks yet of her testimony.
>
> "'I don't know. I don't know. Upstairs? Downstairs? Where was it? I don't know. But I had one beer. That's the only thing I remember,' Trump said of Ford, as he impersonated her on stage.
>
> "'I don't remember,' he said repeatedly, apparently mocking her testimony."

I hear shit like that from my pr*sident and it instantly makes me want to move to any country, wilderness refuge, hollowed-out volcano lair, island cave, or preternaturally commodious marine mammal uterus that will have me.

I mean, what … the … ever-living … fuck?

Were you raised by the dust mites in your dad's fuck pad or something?

Who says shit like this? And what kind of dickless psychopath thinks it's *funny*?

Never mind. I know what kind.

Love,
Pennyfarthing

◆ ◆ ◆

October 3, 2018

- In response to *The New York Times'* bombshell report about his family's tax-dodging, Trump tweets, "The Failing New York Times did something I have never seen done before. They used the concept of 'time value of money' in doing a very old, boring and often told hit piece on me. Added up, this means that 97% of their stories on me are bad. Never recovered from bad election call!"

❖ ❖ ❖

October 5, 2018

- Trump tweets, "The very rude elevator screamers are paid professionals only looking to make Senators look bad. Don't fall for it! Also, look at all of the professionally made identical signs. Paid for by Soros and others. These are not signs made in the basement from love! #Troublemakers"

❖ ❖ ❖

October 6, 2018

- Trump says women are "extremely happy" about Brett Kavanaugh's Supreme Court confirmation.

❖ ❖ ❖

October 8, 2018

- At Brett Kavanaugh's swearing-in ceremony, Trump apologizes to the newest Supreme Court justice.

❖ ❖ ❖

From the Desk of Aldous J. Pennyfarthing
To: Donald Trump, national disgrace

Dear Fucking Moron,

Huh?

> "On behalf of our nation, I would like to apologize to Brett and the entire Kavanaugh family for the terrible pain and suffering you have been forced to endure."

Speak for yourself, shit-nozzle.

Love,
Pennyfarthing

◆ ◆ ◆

October 9, 2018

- UN Ambassador Nikki Haley announces she will leave her post at the end of the year.

◆ ◆ ◆

October 10, 2018

- *USA Today* publishes a Trump op-ed on Medicare for All that's chock-full of easily disproved lies.
- At a Pennsylvania rally, Trump mocks the #MeToo movement, saying, "Every Republican thinks they are going to win Pennsylvania, but I got it. I'd use an expression, you know there's an expression, but under the rules of MeToo I'm not allowed to use that expression anymore, I can't do it."
- ProPublica reports that Trump asked Japanese Prime Minister Shinzo Abe in February 2017 to consider giv-

ing top GOP donor Sheldon Adelson one of the country's casino licenses.

October 11, 2018

- Trump suggests that the scathing *New York Times* op-ed from a member of his own administration may have been written by *The Times* itself: "Even the letter written to the Times, there is a chance — I don't say it's a big chance — but there is a very good chance that that was written by the Times."
- Kanye West visits Trump in the Oval Office.

From the Desk of Aldous J. Pennyfarthing
To: Donald Trump, Rocky Mountain oyster cracker

Dear Fucking Moron,

I watched the video of Kanye West's visit to the Oval Office. It reminded me of that time I shot a fifth of Fireball whiskey into my dick, shoved a Carolina reaper pepper up my ass, smoked a quarter-pound of DMT, and then leapt feet-first into a living Salvador Dali painting while suckling a pair of dyspeptic honey badgers. Except *way* crazier.

Look, every *sane* black person in the country hates you. You've got Kanye Effing West, a man whose EEG chart looks like a 3-year-old's Etch-a-Sketch drawing of two dingoes fucking on a Tilt-A-Whirl.

And what the bejeezus-fuck was this, you sick fucking kook enabler?

"You know, they tried to scare me to not wear this

hat — my own friends. But this hat, it gives me — it gives me power, in a way. You know, my dad and my mom separated, so I didn't have a lot of male energy in my home. And also, I'm married to a family that, you know, not a lot of male energy going on. It's beautiful, though. But there's times where, you know, there's something about — you know, I love Hillary. I love everyone, right? But the campaign 'I'm with her' just didn't make me feel, as a guy, that didn't get to see my dad all the time — like a guy that could play catch with his son. It was something about when I put this hat on, it made me feel like Superman. You made a Superman. That was my — that's my favorite superhero. And you made a Superman cape." — Kanye West, October 11, 2018

That's ... just ... I don't know what.

I mean, it's *sort of* a magical hat, in that it will let the aliens know which of us to sterilize straightaway.

A Superman cape, though? Somehow I missed the Superman comic where he flew to the border, rounded up hundreds of kids in diapers, and kegelspieled them into steel cages.

Also, what superhero's kryptonite is cognitive therapy and a robust cocktail of prescription antipsychotics? That's not any comic book trope I've ever heard of.

You don't need any help looking crazy, man. Next time have Don Jr. or Eric or one of your other ambulant spooge stains on hand with a rhino tranq gun and a straitjacket.

Love,
Pennyfarthing

October 12, 2018

- Trump tweets, "So nice, everyone wants Ivanka Trump to be the new United Nations Ambassador. She would be incredible, but I can already hear the chants of Nepotism! We have great people that want the job."

◆ ◆ ◆

October 13, 2018

- Trump says there will be "severe punishment" if Saudi Arabia is found to be responsible for the death of journalist Jamal Khashoggi.

◆ ◆ ◆

October 15, 2018

- Trump says "rogue killers" might have murdered Jamal Khashoggi.

◆ ◆ ◆

October 16, 2018

- In the wake of journalist Jamal Khashoggi's murder, Trump tweets, "Just spoke with the Crown Prince of Saudi Arabia who totally denied any knowledge of what took place in their Turkish Consulate."
- Trump tweets, "'Federal Judge throws out Stormy Danials lawsuit versus Trump. Trump is entitled to full legal fees.' @FoxNews Great, now I can go after Horseface and her 3rd rate lawyer in the Great State of Texas. She will confirm the letter she signed! She knows nothing about me, a total con!"

From the Desk of Aldous J. Pennyfarthing
To: Donald Trump, grammatical and/or genetic error

Dear Fucking Moron,

Ha ha ha ha!

Wow, you are a real trip ... to a haunted house ... atop a lake of fire ... in an active volcano ... inside Satan's asshole.

You know, spelling Stormy Daniels' name wrong isn't going to convince anyone you didn't bang her. You've misspelled Melania's name, too, and she's actually sort of admitted that you've stuck your miniature candy corn in her.

And, yeah, this bit is unfortunate. For you, anyway:

"She knows nothing about me, a total con!"

Stare at that for a while ... like it's a Zen koan ... like your reputation, peace of mind, and very life depend on attaining some ephemeral spark of enlightenment. Or, if not enlightenment, the closest thing to it you could ever hope to achieve — i.e., a transitory dearth of dumbfuckery.

Got it yet? No?

Come on, sound it out ...

The rest of the class is waiting.

No?

Okay, for the sake of the non-glue-sniffing children, we need to move on.

But seriously, was your mom's uterus a nuclear Superfund site or something? Or did you just freebase too many lead paint chips as a kid?

You know, this is *really* starting to get embarrassing.

For all of us.

Love,
Pennyfarthing

October 17, 2018

> • White House Chief Counsel Don McGahn resigns.

October 18, 2018

> • Trump praises Republican Montana Rep. Greg Gian-forte, who won his seat despite having body-slammed a *Guardian* reporter in May 2017.

From the Desk of Aldous J. Pennyfarthing
To: Donald Trump, angry glop of yam

Dear Fucking Moron,

As your mother would no doubt tell you if she hadn't long ago died of embarrassment, this is fucking appalling:

> "Any guy that can do a body-slam — he's my kind of guy. He's a great guy, tough cookie."

There was a time when criminal assault of a reporter was …

Ah, never mind. You don't care.

And, anyway, these are your fans. As long as you don't show any compassion, you're probably fine. I mean, your supporters are basically Klingons with a few less forehead wrinkles.

That said, once again you're all talk, right? I mean, seriously, if you ever tried to body-slam anything heavier than a Labradoodle, a massive hernia would instantly pop out of your abdomen like a government-recalled Honda airbag.

Just shut the fuck up already, Bone Spurious. No one with an IQ higher than lint is buying your phony tough-guy act anymore.

Love,
Pennyfarthing

October 22, 2018

- Trump tweets that the refugee caravan heading to the U.S.' southern border is a national "emergy."
- At a rally in Houston, Trump says, "You know what I am, I'm a nationalist."

October 23, 2018

- Trump tweets, "Billions of dollars are, and will be, coming into United States coffers because of Tariffs. Great also for negotiations - if a country won't give us a fair Trade Deal, we will institute Tariffs on them. Used or not, jobs and businesses will be created. U.S. respected again!" He fails to mention — again — that American companies and consumers actually pay the tariffs.

October 24, 2018

- An ardent Trump supporter sends pipe bombs to several frequent Trump targets, including CNN, Hillary Clinton, Barack Obama, and George Soros.
- *The New York Times* reports that Trump has been warned against using an unsecured cellphone but does it anyway: "When President Trump calls old friends on one of his iPhones to gossip, gripe or solicit their latest take on how he is doing, American intelligence reports indicate that Chinese spies are often listening — and putting to use invaluable insights into how to best work the president and affect administration policy, current and former American officials said." The report notes that Russian spies routinely eavesdrop on his calls, too.
- At a signing ceremony for the overwhelmingly bipartisan opioid bill Donald Trump somehow claimed had passed with very little Democratic support, Trump first slurs his words while trying to pronounce "ultra-lethal" and then begins to wander away without signing the bill.

From the Desk of Aldous J. Pennyfarthing
To: Donald Trump, comfortable numbnuts

Dear Fucking Moron,

So this was you at one of your *Deliverance* cosplay conventions two weeks ago:

> "I'll soon sign into the law the largest legislative effort in history to address the opioid crisis where just this year we got $6 billion from Congress — thanks to [Sen.] Rob Portman and a lot of others — thank you, Rob — but Rob and so many others

helped. Very little Democrat support."

Very little Democrat support, hmm? (It's "Democratic," by the way, you barn full of Amish-crafted rectal suppositories.)

So here were the final votes on that bill:

Senate: 98-1

House: 393-8

Also, the only "no" vote in the Senate was cast by a Republican.

And would it be rude to point out the keen irony of your slurring your words before wandering away and forgetting to sign an *opioid* bill? Yes, of course it would, which is why I'm doing it.

Love,
Pennyfarthing

October 25, 2018

- Trump tweets, "The so-called experts on Trump over at the New York Times wrote a long and boring article on my cellphone usage that is so incorrect I do not have time here to correct it. I only use Government Phones, and have only one seldom used government cell phone. Story is soooo wrong!"

From the Desk of Aldous J. Pennyfarthing
To: Donald Trump, state secretion

Dear Fucking Moron,

Really?

After all that shit about Hillary's emails, you're walking around with an unsecured cellphone asking people if they know how to convert VHS pee tapes to MPEGs?

Or whatever. I'm just speculating. I should make that clear.

Knowing you, you could be discussing anything from how the code for the nuclear football is the same as your Subway Club Card ID to which Archie Comics character is the most fuckable … Jughead or Mr. Weatherbee.

Either way, it's kind of atrocious, isn't it?

I mean, maybe you're immune to blackmail because everyone already knows you're the most odious slab of protoplasm in the history of the universe. Extorting you would be kind of like trying to blackmail a Country Crock tub full of anthrax.

Still, who knows what government secrets you're spilling like congealed McNugget sauces down your distended drive-in theater screen of a face?

And this after you discussed North Korea strategy in the Mar-a-Lago dining room as God-knows-who shined cellphone lights from *more unsecured phones* onto sensitive documents.

And you of all people made cybersecurity and trustworthiness the leitmotifs of your presidential campaign.

Maybe the government should just give you a Playskool phone that plays nothing but Sean Hannity ass-kissing noises. I can't imagine how you'd ever notice the difference.

Love,
Pennyfarthing

October 26, 2018

- At a North Carolina rally, Trump mocks Rep. Maxine Waters, who had recently been targeted by a pipe bomber who's a big supporter of Trump.
- Trump tweets, "Republicans are doing so well in early voting, and at the polls, and now this 'Bomb' stuff happens and the momentum greatly slows - news not talking politics. Very unfortunate, what is going on. Republicans, go out and vote!"

October 27, 2018

- Hours after a right-wing extremist uses a firearm to murder 11 people at a Pittsburgh-area synagogue, Trump tweets, "Watching the Dodgers/Red Sox final innings. It is amazing how a manager takes out a pitcher who is loose & dominating through almost 7 innings, Rich Hill of Dodgers, and brings in nervous reliever(s) who get shellacked. 4 run lead gone. Managers do it all the time, big mistake!"

From the Desk of Aldous J. Pennyfarthing
To: Donald Trump, seventh-inning blecch

Dear Fucking Moron,

I hope you weren't in the delivery room when your kids were born. I can just see it:

> "Use the forceps! You've gotta grab right onto the head and *squeeze!* HARDER! Now go get the fetus plunger! Put it right on the soft part of the skull! I'm naming this kid Don Jr., and I will *not* let him be a dawdler! Now give 'im to me! What? *Garlic* butter on

my hands?! Who the fuck cares?! Now, now, now!"

So you still don't quite get what a president does, huh? If I wanted to hear half-baked opinions about sports I'd sidle up to strange men at the urinal trough at Lambeau Field. On a day like this, you're supposed to focus on calming nerves and, I don't know, maybe repudiating the virulent racism that's suddenly become more integral to your brand than bad hair and failure.

Why do you think you know everything about topics you haven't even studied —like business ... or politics ... or wearing a tie without looking like a 4-year-old playing dress-up with the clients' clothes at a New Orleans brothel?

Then again, I'd be thrilled if you left your current job to become a Major League Baseball manager. You can even take over my favorite team, the Milwaukee Brewers. That's how much I love this country. You could even put your own stamp on the famous sausage races. Replace the anthropomorphic bratwurst with one of those mini pigs-in-a-blanket they serve at cocktail parties announcing cheaply made Trump-branded dreck. That would be perfect! And for once I could sleep at night content in the knowledge that my home-state baseball team — and not the entire country — is being melted down into a quavering puddle of abject failure and tears.

Love,
Pennyfarthing

◆ ◆ ◆

October 29, 2018

- Following a mass shooting at a Pittsburgh synagogue and an attempted pipe bomb attack that targeted several Trump enemies, Trump tweets, "There is great anger in our Country caused in part by inaccurate, and even fraudulent, reporting of the news. The Fake

> News Media, the true Enemy of the People, must stop the open & obvious hostility & report the news accurately & fairly. That will do much to put out the flame… of Anger and Outrage and we will then be able to bring all sides together in Peace and Harmony. Fake News Must End!"

- Without explanation or evidence, Trump calls Florida Democratic gubernatorial candidate Andrew Gillum "a thief."

October 30, 2018

- Trump claims he can end birthright citizenship, which is enshrined in the 14th Amendment, with an executive order.
- Trump orders 5,200 troops to the U.S.-Mexico border to confront a caravan of hungry immigrants.

From the Desk of Aldous J. Pennyfarthing
To: Donald Trump, king of Shartslyvania

Dear Fucking Moron,

1. You can't just change the Constitution by peeing some neo-Nazi twaddle in the snow with your syphilitic golf pencil.
2. You're sending more than 5,000 troops to the border? Really? Why? Was Ted Cruz spotted near a middle school again?

First things first. Basically you're saying that the American people of 1868, the year the 14th Amendment was ratified, were *not nearly racist enough for your tastes*.

Oh, that was a different time, when black people could get lynched for talking sass to white people. We were way, *way* too enlightened then. Let's turn the clock back to, I don't know, sometime before Sumerian cuneiform writing.

Cuneiform-writin' motherfuckers. Ruined everything.

Oh, but they knew how to build a wall.

Next.

You're really sending 5,000 troops to confront a bunch of befuddled, terrified naïfs in diapers? Here's an idea. You could send *one* soldier to David Vitter's house and save us all a cool $200 million.

Your racism is both horrifying and expensive.

But you knew that already.

Love,
Pennyfarthing

◆ ◆ ◆

October 31, 2018

- Despite backing a lawsuit that would eliminate protections for Americans with preexisting conditions, Trump tweets, "Republicans will protect people with pre-existing conditions far better than the Dems!"

November 3, 2018

- *The Washington Post* reports that the cost of Trump's troop deployment to the U.S.-Mexico border "could climb well above $200 million by the end of 2018."

- Trump tweets, "Landing in Montana now - at least everybody admits that my lines and crowds are far bigger than Barack Obama's..."

November 5, 2018

- Trump tweets, "So funny to see the CNN Fake Suppression Polls and false rhetoric. Watch for real results Tuesday. We are lucky CNN's ratings are so low. Don't fall for the Suppression Game. Go out & VOTE. Remember, we now have perhaps the greatest Economy (JOBS) in the history of our Country!"

November 6, 2018

- Democrats pick up dozens of seats in the House and several governorships in the midterms. Republicans retain control of the Senate.

November 7, 2018

- After Trump berates CNN's Jim Acosta for questions he didn't like, the White House revokes the reporter's press credentials.
- Attorney General Jeff Sessions resigns at Trump's request. Trump names Sessions' chief of staff, Matt Whitaker, acting attorney general.
- In a column for Politico, former Trump Plaza Hotel & Casino president Jack O'Donnell writes, "I saw [Trump] treat black people and minorities as inferior. I heard him say vulgar, bigoted things and I rebuked

him for them. But he did not quit. Indeed, he has continued it to this day."

- Trump claims the midterm results were "very close to complete victory" for Republicans, even though the party suffered major losses nearly everywhere except the U.S. Senate.

◆ ◆ ◆

From the Desk of Aldous J. Pennyfarthing
To: Donald Trump, inveterate fuckup

Dear Fucking Moron,

Whew! Busy day in the worlds of politics and pants-shitting cray-cray.

But I suppose the lede is you getting your spongy circus peanut skull kicked in by Nancy Pelosi and her Inglourious Basterds.

Nice Monty Python Black Knight impression, by the way.

What else do you want to gaslight us with this morning? Did you solve the Einstein-Podolsky-Rosen paradox while taking a dump at Carl's Jr.? Have the monkeys that flew out of your ass last Tuesday discovered the Higgs boson? Did you sequence the human genome with the Spider-Man Legos in your Happy Meal?

By "very close to complete victory" I can only assume you nearly hunted down and killed the chicken that's been beating you at tic-tac-toe, because what the fuck else could you be talking about?

The *election*?

No. Just no.

Dude, you sound like Hitler in April 1945 telling Eva Braun how he's going to turn the bunker into a really cool AirBnB.

Oh, and just because you start revoking reporters' press credentials doesn't mean they're suddenly going to start reporting that you slew the Gorgon on Unicorn Island.

Then again, Sean Hannity might — if you let him out of his gimp costume.

Love,
Pennyfarthing

November 9, 2018

- After naming Matt Whitaker acting attorney general, Trump says, "I don't know Matt Whitaker."
- After arriving in Paris, Trump tweets, "President Macron of France has just suggested that Europe build its own military in order to protect itself from the U.S., China and Russia. Very insulting, but perhaps Europe should first pay its fair share of NATO, which the U.S. subsidizes greatly!"
- After British Prime Minister Theresa May calls Trump to congratulate him over his nearly nonexistent election wins, Trump reportedly berates her over Brexit, Iran, and U.S.-European trade deals.

◆ ◆ ◆

November 10, 2018

- As deadly wildfires burn out of control in California, Trump tweets, "There is no reason for these massive, deadly and costly forest fires in California except that forest management is so poor. Billions of dollars are given each year, with so many lives lost, all because of gross mismanagement of the forests. Remedy now, or no more Fed payments!"

- Trump skips a ceremony at the Aisne-Marne American Cemetery and Memorial in Belleau, France, because it rained. The ceremony commemorated the 100th anniversary of the end of World War I.

November 11, 2018

- Trump decides not to visit Arlington National Cemetery on Veterans Day because he is "extremely busy on calls for the country."
- Of Trump's presidency, Gen. Michael Hayden, a former director of both the National Security Agency and the CIA, tweets, "[W]e are off the scale dishonoring the office."

November 12, 2018

- Without citing evidence, Trump claims the ballots for Florida's gubernatorial and Senate elections were "massively infected" and says election officials "Must go with Election Night!" Naturally, both Republicans were ahead on election night before ballots were done being counted.

November 13, 2018

- *The Los Angeles Times* reports that Trump "has retreated into a cocoon of bitterness and resentment" since the midterms.

From the Desk of Aldous J. Pennyfarthing
To: Donald Trump, dick-whistling git

Dear Fucking Moron,

You know, you can make a fort out of your couch cushions and live there happily for days, subsisting entirely on stored fat and carpet detritus. How do I know this? Well, I have such a fort, and it's what we affectionately refer to around here as the Winter Pennyfarthing Manse. Occasionally I'll leave the house in a giant plastic hamster ball, but only to get beer, weed, and some cockroach sauce (the affectionate term I've adopted for pretty much anything Kraft produces that has an actual melting point).

It's pretty much been my go-to coping mechanism since November 2016. Because apparently no reputable doctor will put a healthy person in a four-year coma no matter how many psychologist's notes and pallets of Snapple you give her.

So for once I understand what the fuck you're talking about. I've been there, man. Because of you. But still. I wouldn't wish it on my worst enemy ... who is also you, come to think of it.

So cheer up, Eeyore. There's a big, bright world out there just waiting to be destroyed by your unique mix of phlegmatic ineptitude and diabolical evil.

No one else is going to do it. No one else could, little one.

Love,
Pennyfarthing

November 14, 2018

- Deputy National Security Adviser Mira Ricardel is forced to leave her job after an apparent conflict with Melania Trump.
- *Vanity Fair* reports that Trump skipped the World War I commemoration ceremony at Aisne-Marne American Cemetery because of his hair.

From the Desk of Aldous J. Pennyfarthing
To: Donald Trump, Velveeta-eating surrender monkey

Dear Fucking Moron,

Dear God.

You really don't understand how to do this job, do you?

Needless to say, though, I love this explanation, from Gabriel Sherman at *Vanity Fair*:

> "Trump skipped attending a rain-soaked ceremony at the Aisne-Marne American Cemetery to honor the Battle of Belleau Wood. When his absence became a scandal, the White House said the decision had been made because Marine One reportedly could not fly in the rain, and Secret Service did not want Trump traveling by motorcade. One Republican briefed on the internal discussions said the real reason Trump did not want to go was because there would be no tent to stand under. 'He was worried his hair was going to get messed up in the rain,' the source said. '[John] Bolton and everyone was telling him this was a big mistake.' A former administration official said Trump hates being outside in wet conditions. 'What I honestly think? He woke up and said, 'It's pouring rain. This is a joke and I'm not

doing this.'"

Yeah, I get it. I mean, having to go to some ridiculous ceremony for some stupid fucking war you've never even heard of is a huge drag. You've got tweetering to do! How will people know whether or not the Mueller investigation is a witch hunt ... or how many Angry Democrats are on Mueller's team this week? What if one of the Democrats isn't quite as angry as before? You'll want to correct the record immediately because, for God's sake, you're the president! And the president can't simply be an endless font of rancid, semi-gelatinous donkey shit with no discernible point. How would that look?

These people are living in the past! You've got your eye squarely on the future. I mean, the McRib always comes back eventually, right?

Love,
Pennyfarthing

November 15, 2018

- The Daily Beast reports that Trump "has repeatedly — and sometimes for a sustained period of time — made fun of [Sean] Hannity's interviewing skills, usually zeroing in on the low-quality laziness of the host's questions."

November 17, 2018

- While touring areas devastated by California's wildfires, Trump says, "I was with the president of Finland and he said, 'We have a much different ... we're a forest nation,' he called it a forest nation. And they spend a lot of time on raking and cleaning and doing things and they don't have any problem." Trump also refers to Paradise, California, where much of the damage was done, as "Pleasure."

◆ ◆ ◆

From the Desk of Aldous J. Pennyfarthing
To: Donald Trump, Woodsy Bowel

Dear Fucking Moron,

You know, if you had said Finland doesn't have a wildfire problem because its enchanted forest pixies dutifully smother all flames with their magick faerie dongs, it would have been at least twice as believable.

The president of Finland didn't tell you that the whole country pitches in on Saturdays to rake the country's forest floors. How do I know that? Because only your febrile, fragrant dunghill of a brain could ever come up with such a thing.

Also, he *said* he never said it.

So should we believe the president of Finland or the guy who doesn't know how to close an umbrella and still thinks we have invisible planes? That's a real head-scratcher, man.

Of course, Finland does have a very real and successful universal health care system and an innovative, progressive education system that's the envy of the world, but why pay attention to any of that when we've got chores to do?

Also, if you can find one reputable scientist who thinks California's wildfire problem boils down to a lack of forest raking, I will rip my still-beating heart out of my chest with a Swiss army knife leather awl and eat it in front of my mother like a Del Taco chimichanga at bar time.

Love,
Pennyfarthing

◆ ◆ ◆

November 18, 2018

- The actual president of the United States tweets, "So funny to see little Adam Schitt (D-CA) talking about the fact that Acting Attorney General Matt Whitaker was not approved by the Senate, but not mentioning the fact that Bob Mueller (who is highly conflicted) was not approved by the Senate!"

◆ ◆ ◆

November 19, 2018

- During an interview with Fox News' Chris Wallace, Trump dismisses Admiral William McRaven, a critic of Trump, as a "Hillary backer and an Obama backer." When Wallace notes that McRaven was in charge of the successful raid that killed Osama bin Laden, Trump says, "Wouldn't it have been nice if we got Osama bin Laden a lot sooner than that? Wouldn't it have been nice?"
- *The Washington Post* reports that Ivanka Trump used a personal email account to conduct official White House business. She later claims she was somehow not familiar with the rules barring such activity.

◆ ◆ ◆

November 20, 2018

- *The New York Times* reports that Trump wanted to

order the DOJ to prosecute Hillary Clinton and former FBI director James Comey.

- Trump submits written answers to questions Robert Mueller had about Russian interference in the 2016 presidential election.
- Trump says he "can't imagine" anyone but Trump as *Time*'s Person of the Year. Apparently, *Time* can imagine it, as he was later snubbed for the "honor."
- Trump gives Saudi Arabia a pass in the apparent murder of journalist Jamal Khashoggi, writing, "King Salman and Crown Prince Mohammad bin Salman vigorously deny any knowledge of the planning or execution of the murder of Mr. Khashoggi."

From the Desk of Aldous J. Pennyfarthing
To: Donald Trump, ruthless prick-traitor

Dear Fucking Moron,

Okay, after you're done sucking the cock of every *living* dictator on the planet, maybe your buddy Vlad can pry open Lenin's glass coffin so you can polish his tyrannical todger as well.

Bone saws, dude. Fucking *bone saws*. What part of "bone" and "saws" are you not getting?

So the CIA says the Saudi government was involved in killing Jamal Khashoggi — a U.S. resident and *Washington Post* journalist, by the way — but you prefer the story of the people who have been implicated in the crime they're denying.

This is a good one, too:

> "It could very well be that the crown prince had knowledge of this tragic event — maybe he did and maybe he didn't!"

Wow, you really *are* tough on crime!

Anyway, it's refreshing to have a president who's so guileless, so trusting, so magnanimous, and so generous of spirit that he sees only the best in peop …

Oh, good God, what the fuck is this?

> "Mayor Koch has stated that hate and rancor should be removed from our hearts. I do not think so. I want to hate these muggers and murderers. They should be forced to suffer and, when they kill, they should be executed for their crimes. They must serve as examples so that others will think long and hard before committing a crime or an act of violence. Yes, Mayor Koch, I want to hate these murderers and I always will."

Yeah, that's part of an ad you took out in 1989, back when your soul was only just beginning to putrefy. You called for the execution of the Central Park Five, a group of African-American teenagers who had been accused of beating and raping a female jogger in Central Park.

Oh, but that was way, *way* different, of course.

They were innocent.

Love,
Pennyfarthing

November 21, 2018

- After Chief Justice John Roberts rebukes Trump over Trump's partisan attacks on federal judges, Trump tweets, "Sorry Chief Justice John Roberts, but you do indeed have 'Obama judges,' and they have a much different point of view than the people who are charged with the safety of our country. It would be great if the 9th Circuit was indeed an 'independent judiciary,' but if it is why...... are so many opposing view (on Border and Safety) cases filed there, and why are a vast number of those cases overturned."

November 22, 2018

- Trump confirms that he's authorized the troops he sent to the southern border to use lethal force, if "necessary."
- Trump appears to contradict the CIA's finding that Saudi Crown Prince Mohammed bin Salman was responsible for journalist Jamal Khasshogi's death, saying agency officials "have feelings certain ways."
- Trump uses his Thanksgiving call to the troops as an excuse to grind political axes and brag about himself.
- Asked what he's thankful for this year, Trump says "for having a great family and for having made a tremendous difference in this country."

From the Desk of Aldous J. Pennyfarthing
To: Donald Trump, cosmic ingrate

Dear Fucking Moron,

Can you help me? Where can I find the "jaw dropping below my flaccid Ron Jeremy dick" emoji? I know I've seen it somewhere before. Maybe there's a keyboard shortcut?

It's *Thanksgiving*, you Wienermobile full of blobfish farts.

Not everything is about *you*.

People share delicious home-cooked meals, sit by the family hearth with their loved ones, and bask in the abiding spirit of gemütlichkeit. They don't thank themselves for *themselves*.

Can you take one second out of each day to stop tonguing your own taint and focus on the country you pretend to be running?

For *Christ's* sake.

Love,
Pennyfarthing

November 23, 2018

- A New York state judge rules that the New York attorney general's civil suit against the Trump Foundation can proceed.

November 25, 2018

- Border patrol agents fire tear gas at migrants, some of them children in diapers, at a U.S.-Mexico border crossing near San Diego.
- Axios reports that Trump twice tried to convince Iraq's prime minister to hand over the country's oil.

November 26, 2018

- Robert Mueller states in a court filing that Paul Manafort, Trump's former campaign chair, breached his plea agreement by lying to the special counsel's office.

- GM announces it will lay off 14,700 employees and close up to five plants in North America.
- Outgoing GOP congresswoman Mia Love slams Trump in her concession speech.
- Trump tweeters a tweet suggesting the U.S. government should start its own news network to compete internationally with CNN.

◆ ◆ ◆

From the Desk of Aldous J. Pennyfarthing
To: Donald Trump, plug-ugly mingebag

Dear Fucking Moron,

Okay, this is a really fucking stupid idea, for a couple of reasons:

> "While CNN doesn't do great in the United States based on ratings, outside of the U.S. they have very little competition. Throughout the world, CNN has a powerful voice portraying the United States in an unfair.... and false way. Something has to be done, including the possibility of the United States starting our own Worldwide Network to show the World the way we really are, GREAT!"

And here's what's so fucking stupid about it:

1. This already pretty much exists. It's called Voice of America, and it's been around since 1942. I know your grasp of American history is pretty tenuous, but I figured this out in about five seconds, and I'm not even president. Also, stop telling your hookers to dress up as Dolley Madison and meet you in the Lincoln Bedroom. That's a glaring anachronism. Get it together, for fuck's sake.
2. Since you're obviously not talking about Voice of America, you must be imagining — oh, I don't know

—a state-run propaganda outlet like Pravda or North Korean state TV. And I can only assume they'll consistently find the precise 1.3-degree camera angle in which you somehow don't look like Jabba the Hutt's placenta.

Get this through your hair weave: The media don't exist to flatter you and fluff your micro-dong. If you don't like how they report on your presidency, stop being such a focking arse-chapeau.

Love,
Pennyfarthing

◆ ◆ ◆

November 27, 2018

- Trump retweets a graphic showing several of his political foes behind bars and asking, "When do the trials for treason begin?"
- *The Washington Post* reports that Trump thought former Federal Reserve Chair Janet Yellen was too short to run the Fed.
- During an interview with *The Washington Post*, Trump says he regrets nominating Jerome Powell as Fed chair, claiming the Fed shouldn't be raising interest rates so rapidly: "They're making a mistake because I have a gut, and my gut tells me more sometimes than anybody else's brain can ever tell me."

From the Desk of Aldous J. Pennyfarthing
To: Donald Trump, financial lizard

Dear Fucking Moron,

Let's get one thing straight, you oafish piss balloon. The only thing your gut ever told you that made a whit of sense was "another large pitcher of creamy ranch sauce for the table, please."

Your "gut" allowed you to bankrupt a casino company, which is basically the business equivalent of getting your tongue stuck to a frozen light pole.

Your gut is worthless, and your brain is even worthlesser. The only way your guts could ever be of use in decision-making is if a voodoo priestess scattered them on a shrine and read them like chicken entrails.

And Janet Yellen is too short to run the Fed?

Dude, she was in charge of keeping the economy stimulated, not your ropy wang. She's not a Miss Teen USA contestant you're trying to screw. Who the fuck cares how tall she is?

Remember how you were initially reluctant to hire John Bolton because you didn't like his mustache? Apparently Bolton's unblemished decades-long record of cartoonish evil eventually won you over — and the fact that he looks like Wilford Brimley's necrotic goiter was not nearly as important to you as his baleful death stare. Guess if you're the most Machiavellian shitheel on the planet you get a pass.

Sorry, Janet. You must be this tall to ride Li'l Donnie's economic roller coaster. Better luck next time.

Love,
Pennyfarthing

November 28, 2018

- · Trump indicates he would be willing to shut down the government over funding for his southern border wall.

◆ ◆ ◆

November 29, 2018

- Robert Mueller files a court document stating that Michael Cohen lied to Congress about Trump's plans to build a Trump Tower in Moscow. Trump had repeatedly stated during the presidential campaign that he had nothing to do with Russia. Trump responds to the news by calling Cohen a "weak person."
- Trump cancels a meeting with Vladimir Putin scheduled for the G20 summit, supposedly over Ukrainian ships Russia had seized.

◆ ◆ ◆

November 30, 2018

- In response to the news that Trump had pursued a Trump Tower Moscow for much longer than he had previously acknowledged, he tweets, "Oh, I get it! I am a very good developer, happily living my life, when I see our Country going in the wrong direction (to put it mildly). Against all odds, I decide to run for President & continue to run my business-very legal & very cool, talked about it on the campaign trail ..."
- Vladimir Putin and Saudi Crown Prince Mohammad Bin Salman share a laugh and a high-five at the G20 summit.

◆ ◆ ◆

December 1, 2018

- Trump announces he's reached an "incredible" trade

deal with China. Three days later, the White House plays down the announcement and JP Morgan issues a trading note that says, "It doesn't seem like anything was actually agreed to at the dinner and White House officials are contorting themselves into pretzels to reconcile Trump's tweets (which seem if not completely fabricated then grossly exaggerated) with reality."

· Every G20 leader except Trump signs onto a declaration supporting the global fight against climate change.

December 2, 2018

· Russian state media mocks Trump in the wake of the G20 summit. TV host Evgeny Popov criticizes Trump's decision to cancel his meeting with Putin: "Just a few minutes earlier he said that now is a good time to meet. ... What kind of a man is this — first he says it will happen, then it won't — are we just supposed to wait until he gets reelected to start communicating with America? This is just foolishness, he seems to be an unbalanced person."

December 3, 2018

· In a tweet that many observers see as a clear example of witness tampering, Trump writes, "'I will never testify against Trump.' This statement was recently made by Roger Stone, essentially stating that he will not be forced by a rogue and out of control prosecutor to make up lies and stories about 'President Trump.'

Nice to know that some people still have 'guts!'"

December 4, 2018

- GOP senators emerge from a CIA briefing on the death of journalist Jamal Khashoggi convinced that Saudi Crown Prince Mohammed bin Salman ordered the killing. In stark contrast to Trump's "maybe he did, maybe he didn't" stance on MBS' role, Sen. Bob Corker says, "If the crown prince went in front of a jury, he would be convicted in 30 minutes."
- In a court filing, Robert Mueller recommends a light sentence for Michael Flynn based on the substantial assistance he gave investigators looking into the Trump-Russia affair. The sentencing memo reveals that Flynn sat for 19 interviews with Mueller's team.
- After Trump calls himself "Tariff Man" in a tweet, the Dow drops nearly 800 points.

From the Desk of Aldous J. Pennyfarthing
To: Donald Trump, Jack-off all trades

Dear Fucking Moron,

I used to think a million monkeys banging on typewriters could come up with better economic policies than you could. Then I figured one monkey with a stylus and a can of Play-Doh could do the job. Now I think if a monkey ate a box of typewriter ribbons, waited a couple of days, and then flung its poo at Larry Kudlow's forehead, we'd finally get the sober, reasoned trade policy we all deserve.

So what's this *crottin de cheval*, pray tell?

"....I am a Tariff Man. When people or countries come in to raid the great wealth of our Nation, I want them to pay for the privilege of doing so. It will always be the best way to max out our economic power. We are right now taking in $billions in Tariffs. MAKE AMERICA RICH AGAIN"

You know, I always have thought of you as a superhero — Dung Beetle Man: an ordinary, mild-mannered dung beetle who was bitten by a radioactive man. Because, you know, you can roll gargantuan balls of feces many times your size. You're the Sisyphus of shit, in other words.

Tariff Man kind of fits, though.

Except for the fact that you have no idea how tariffs work. Other than that, it's perfect.

You see, foreign countries don't pay our tariffs; our own people do. So, to extend the superhero analogy, this is sort of like Captain America using his shield to bake meatloaf in because he doesn't know it does anything else.

That is, you're a fucking idiot who has no idea he's a fucking idiot.

And that's your other amazing superhero power, isn't it, Dunning-Kruger Man?

Love,
Pennyfarthing

◆ ◆ ◆

December 5, 2018

- Trump attends President George H.W. Bush's funeral and appears to pout through most of it.

December 6, 2018

- In an interview with CBS' Bob Schieffer, former Secretary of State Rex Tillerson says Trump is "undis-
ciplined, doesn't like to read, doesn't read briefing reports, [and] doesn't like to get into the details of a lot
of things, but rather just kind of says, 'This is what I
believe.'" The next day, Trump tweets, "Mike Pompeo
is doing a great job, I am very proud of him. His predecessor, Rex Tillerson, didn't have the mental capacity
needed. He was dumb as a rock and I couldn't get rid of
him fast enough. He was lazy as hell."

December 7, 2018

- Trump announces he'll nominate former George H.W.
Bush AG William Barr as attorney general and former
Fox & Friends host Heather Nauert as ambassador to
the UN.
- Following the release of sentencing recommenda-
tions for Michael Cohen, in which Cohen admitted to
paying off Stormy Daniels "in coordination with and
at the direction of Individual-1" (i.e., Trump), Trump
tweets, "Totally clears the President. Thank you!"

From the Desk of Aldous J. Pennyfarthing
To: Donald Trump, Individual-dung

Dear Fucking Moron,

I realize I've made fun of your looks a lot in these letters. Maybe that's not fair. After all, basically every picture of me looks like the last known photo of a guy who got drunk and fell off a cruise ship. So I'm being pretty hypocritical here. But to be fair, I mock your looks only for the noblest of reasons (i.e., because you're a huge asshole).

But ... at least I'm not an intractably corrupt idiot who also happens to look like ...

Sorry, I'm doing it again. I was going to dredge up some esoteric modifier and then promptly append an illiberal scurrility like, I don't know, "cheddarwurst" ... but, again, that's hardly fair. Because you look more like a braunschweiger, honestly.

What were we talking about?

Oh, yeah. This:

> "During the campaign, Cohen played a central role in two similar schemes to purchase the rights to stories—each from women who claimed to have had an affair with Individual-1—so as to suppress the stories and thereby prevent them from influencing the election. With respect to both payments, Cohen acted with the intent to influence the 2016 presidential election. Cohen coordinated his actions with one or more members of the campaign, including through meetings and phone calls, about the fact, nature, and timing of the payments. (PSR ¶ 51). In particular, and as Cohen himself has now admitted, with respect to both payments, he acted in coordination with and at the direction of Individual-1."

And this:

> "Totally clears the President. Thank you!"

Huh? President of what? You can't possibly be talking about yourself. Can you?

Or are you trying to pretend you're not Individual-1? Because ... uh ... this "president of the United States" thing is the worst secret identity, like, ever. No matter what you do and how many American flags you dry-hump into humiliated ribbons of polyester and bottom-shelf baby batter, all I can see is the guy who tacked his name onto a fake university in order to bilk people out of their life savings and then lied about it.

That guy is Individual-1 to a T. And he was just implicated in two possible felonies.

Love,
Pennyfarthing

◆ ◆ ◆

December 8, 2018

- *Forbes* reports that Trump appears to be swindling his campaign contributors for profit by allowing his companies to charge rent to his campaign.
- After Sen. Richard Blumenthal criticizes him, Trump calls Blumenthal "Da Nang Dick" in a tweet.

From the Desk of Aldous J. Pennyfarthing
To: Donald Trump, Ho Chi Minge

Dear Fucking Moron,

Hmm, I just assumed Da Nang Dick was something you caught during your own personal Vietnam.

Watch the projection there, STDonnie.

By the way, just to refresh your moldering crack house of a memory, here's what you were responding to:

> "Prosecutors in the Southern District of New York, independent of the special counsel investigation, believe that Donald Trump committed a felony that enabled him or at least helped him to become president. Covering up those payments is part of what was done, part of the conspiracy in which Donald Trump is an unindicted co-conspirator."

And your droll riposte:

> "Watched Da Nang Dick Blumenthal on television spewing facts almost as accurate as his bravery in Vietnam (which he never saw). As the bullets whizzed by Da Nang Dicks head, as he was saving soldiers.... left and right, he then woke up from his dream screaming that HE LIED. Next time I go to Vietnam I will ask 'the Dick' to travel with me!"

My piddling dream for America is that we'll one day have a president whose unspeakably callow third-grade insults employ proper grammar.

It's really not too much to ask.

By the way, you calling another human being a cowardly liar is like Jeffrey Dahmer complaining about the guy at Olive Garden taking unfair advantage of the bottomless breadsticks.

Anyway, can't wait for the next Twitter bon mot, Li'l Donnie! Hope it involves boom-booms or pee-pees. That's your wheelhouse, my man.

Love,
Pennyfarthing

December 10, 2018

- *The Washington Post* announces that is has created a new fact-check rating, the Bottomless Pinocchio, to address Trump's habit of continually repeating already debunked lies.

December 11, 2018

- Trump tweets, "People do not yet realize how much of the Wall, including really effective renovation, has already been built. If the Democrats do not give us the votes to secure our Country, the Military will build the remaining sections of the Wall. They know how important it is!"
- In an Oval Office meeting with Nancy Pelosi and Chuck Schumer, Trump says, "I am proud to shut down the government for border security, Chuck. ... I will take the mantle. I will be the one to shut it down. I'm not going to blame you for it."

December 12, 2018

- Former Trump lawyer and "fixer" Michael Cohen is sentenced to three years in prison for lying to Congress and committing campaign finance violations.
- *The National Enquirer* admits it conspired with Trump to bury news of his extramarital affairs prior to the 2016 election. It did so by buying exclusive rights to stories and then spiking them as part of a scheme

called "catch and kill."

From the Desk of Aldous J. Pennyfarthing
To: Donald Trump, dumbass peckerwood

Dear Fucking Moron,

You know, in more innocent times this scandal would have lasted at least as long as the furor over Barack Obama's tan suit, but we have to clear out some head space for the next revelation, which could be anything from insurance fraud to finding out Putin has a tape of you blending endangered species yogurt smoothies in your Vitamix while you get your dick sucked by a drugged Roswell alien.

Somehow, though, I have a feeling Jerry Falwell Jr. will say this proves that God handpicked you for the presidency. Because that's just how God rolls. Jesus needed someone to cut child health insurance funding and, hey, if that guy likes to bang porn stars and lie about it? Gravy.

Then again, I do see God's hand in all this — because the publisher of the *National Enquirer*, who covered up these malefactions, is named David Pecker.

The puns just write themselves. It's almost not fair — like playing tetherball against drunk crickets.

"Trump's Pecker revealed!"

See? Too easy. So I'll stop now.

"Trump caught by his Pecker!"

Sorry. It's like eating chips. You can't stop at just one.

Love,
Pennyfarthing

December 13, 2018

- *The New York Times* reports that federal prosecutors are investigating Trump's inaugural fund.

December 14, 2018

- In an interview with *Good Morning America*, Michael Cohen claims Trump directed him to make hush money payments to Stormy Daniels and Karen McDougal.
- Chris Christie withdraws his name from consideration for Trump's open chief of staff position.
- Trump announces via Twitter that he's named Office of Management and Budget Director Mick Mulvaney acting chief of staff.

December 15, 2018

- Trump announces Interior Secretary Ryan Zinke will leave his position at the end of the year. Zinke departs under a cloud of scandal.

December 16, 2018

- Trump tweets, "Remember, Michael Cohen only became a 'Rat' after the FBI did something which was absolutely unthinkable & unheard of until the Witch

Hunt was illegally started. They BROKE INTO AN AT-TORNEY'S OFFICE! Why didn't they break into the DNC to get the Server, or Crooked's office?"

- Trump suggests the government should monitor *Saturday Night Live*'s content, tweeting, "A REAL scandal is the one sided coverage, hour by hour, of networks like NBC & Democrat spin machines like Saturday Night Live. It is all nothing less than unfair news coverage and Dem commercials. Should be tested in courts, can't be legal? Only defame & belittle! Collusion?"

◆ ◆ ◆

From the Desk of Aldous J. Pennyfarthing
To: Donald Trump, bill of frights

Dear Fucking Moron,

Jesus Pogo-hoppin' Christ, what the fuck is wrong with you?

Well, you *did* tell us that we'd get tired of all the whining. I think that's what you said, anyway.

So I haven't watched SNL in a while. Let me guess. Did they do a five-year-long sketch about how your birth certificate is a forgery, even though they had zero evidence to prove it? Because why the fuck else would you care? It's a fucking comedy show that's brutally skewered every goddamn president since Gerald Ford.

So the actual president of the United States has no idea how the First Amendment works. Or doesn't care.

Apparently, you were either lying your ass off when you took the oath of office (likely) or are as dumb as a sack of gently used alpaca sharts (much more likely).

Of course, it's always boggled my mind that anyone has ever

taken you seriously on any topic outside your areas of expertise, which are pretty much limited to yourself, what you want to eat next, and people who have crossed you.

For example, the late Wharton professor William Kelley reportedly said, "Donald Trump was the dumbest goddamn student I ever had." And the guy who ghostwrote *The Art of the Deal* thinks you're a fucking moron with the attention span of an eyelash mite.

So I get that you don't know things.

But our constitutionally protected right to free speech (especially to *political* speech!) is fundamental. It protects us from — gee, I don't know — becoming a tyrannical state. That you don't get that — as *president* of the *United States* — is pretty fucking appalling.

Then again, what else is new?

Love,
Pennyfarthing

December 18, 2018

- Trump agrees to shut down the Donald J. Trump Foundation in the wake of a lawsuit filed by New York's attorney general that alleged "persistently illegal conduct" at the foundation.

December 19, 2018

- Trump announces he will pull all U.S. troops out of Syria, claiming, "We have won against ISIS. We have beaten them and we have beaten them badly."

December 20, 2018

- Secretary of Defense James Mattis resigns following Trump's Syria decision. His resignation letter is widely seen as a rebuke of Trump's policies and leadership style.
- After minimal consultation with his advisers, Trump announces he will reduce the number of U.S. troops in Afghanistan.
- Trump sets the stage for a government shutdown after he announces that any spending bill must include money for his border wall.

December 21, 2018

- In a tweet touting his proposal for a southern border wall, Trump says, "I know tech better than anyone."
- Bloomberg reports that Trump discussed firing Fed Chair Jerome Powell over the central bank's interest rate hikes.
- Axios reports that Trump was reportedly furious after video surfaced in which his new acting chief of staff, Mick Mulvaney, said, "Yes, I am supporting Donald Trump, but I'm doing so despite the fact that I think he's a terrible human being."

December 22, 2018

- After the government is shut down over an impasse over border wall funding, Nancy Pelosi and Chuck

Schumer release a joint statement saying, "Republicans control the House, the Senate, and the White House. But instead of honoring his responsibility to the American people, President Trump threw a temper tantrum and convinced House Republicans to push our nation into a destructive Trump Shutdown in the middle of the holiday season. President Trump has said more than 25 times that he wanted a shutdown and now he has gotten what he wanted."

- *The New York Times* reports that "the president has told associates he feels 'totally and completely abandoned,' as one put it, complaining that no one is on his side and that many around him have ulterior motives. That extends even to his son-in-law, Jared Kushner, who was credited for helping push through the criminal justice bill, praise that Mr. Trump took note of.

December 23, 2018

- Trump announces that Secretary of Defense James Mattis will leave the administration on January 1, two months ahead of schedule. Trump was reportedly irritated by Mattis' resignation letter, which was seen as a thinly veiled criticism of the pr*sident. Trump appoints former Boeing executive Patrick Shanahan as acting defense secretary.

December 24, 2018

- Following Trump's attacks on Fed Chair Jerome Powell and Treasury Secretary Steven Mnuchin's bizarre calls to six bank executives, the Dow Jones plunges

653 points.
- Trump self-pity-tweets about being alone in the White House on Christmas Eve.
- While fielding calls from children calling into the NORAD Santa tracker, Trump asks one kid, "Are you still a believer in Santa? ... Because at 7 it's marginal, right?"

◆ ◆ ◆

From the Desk of Aldous J. Pennyfarthing
To: Donald Trump, Satan's go-to ass loofah

Dear Fucking Moron,

Merry Christmas, you billowing, Brobdingnagian berm of blushing baboon bits.

See? I didn't say "happy holidays." Because it's safe to say wh'ever the fuck you want now, so long as it starts with "Merry Christmas."

Merry Christmas, movie house! Merry Christmas, Emporium! Merry Christmas, you wonderful old Building and Loan! Merry Christmas, Mr. Potter! Merry Christmas, Trump Tower! Merry Christmas, Cthulhu! Merry Christmas, Flying Spaghetti Monster! Merry Christmas, Satan's glorious, luminescent asshole!

And Jesus Christ, now you're telling kids there's no Santa Claus? I guess that's better than waking up the day after election night and finding out Donald Trump is president-elect, but still. I mean, suddenly you don't know how to lie? That's like Superman faking a limp because he doesn't feel like pulling a drowning toddler out of a river.

Seriously, you are the shittiest shit-slurping shitbird on Shit Island. Plus, *you* think North Korea is denuclearizing and *you're* 72 fucking years old, so who's the real idiot here?

Also ...

> "I am all alone (poor me) in the White House waiting for the Democrats to come back and make a deal on desperately needed Border Security. At some point the Democrats not wanting to make a deal will cost our Country more money than the Border Wall we are all talking about. Crazy!"

Oh, go stick your Silly Putty scrotum in an off-brand waffle iron. No one fucking cares.

Happy holidays.

Love,
Pennyfarthing

◆ ◆ ◆

December 25, 2018

- Trump says that only an Olympic champion could get over his proposed border wall.

◆ ◆ ◆

December 26, 2018

- While visiting the troops in Iraq, Trump lies to them about their own salaries. According to *The Washington Post*, "The president also told a number of falsehoods to the troops during his speech. He said that he had given the troops a 10 percent pay raise and that the forces had not received a pay raise in more than 10 years. The sizable pay raise Trump authorized earlier this year, however, amounted to 2.6 percent, not 10 percent, and troops have received a pay raise every year for decades."

- Two daughters of the doctor who diagnosed Trump with bone spurs say he did it as a favor to Trump's father, Fred, who owned the building where the doctor practiced. The diagnosis allowed Trump to secure a deferment from serving in Vietnam.

◆ ◆ ◆

From the Desk of Aldous J. Pennyfarthing
To: Donald Trump, pusillanimous fart golem

Dear Fucking Moron,

So the guy who diagnosed your "bone spurs" was in your dad's pocket, huh? Since you'd likely napalm your knickers 500 shades of brown if you played Call of Duty without your binky or a Babybjörn full of Xanax, it's probably just as well.

I mean, you act tough, but then there's this, from a 2008 interview you did with Howard Stern:

> "I was at Mar-a-Lago and we had this incredible ball, the Red Cross Ball, in Palm Beach, Florida. And we had the Marines. And the Marines were there, and it was terrible because all these rich people, they're there to support the Marines, but they're really there to get their picture in the *Palm Beach Post*. So you have all these really rich people, and a man, about 80 years old — very wealthy man, a lot of people didn't like him — he fell off the stage. So what happens is, this guy falls off right on his face, hits his head, and I thought he died. And you know what I did? I said, 'Oh my God, that's disgusting,' and I turned away. I couldn't, you know, he was right in front of me and I turned away. I didn't want to touch him. He's bleeding all over the place, I felt terrible. You know, beautiful marble floor, didn't look like it.

It changed color. Became very red. And you have this poor guy, 80 years old, laying on the floor unconscious, and all the rich people are turning away."

Holy shit, Little Lord Fauntleroy. You couldn't risk getting a little blood on your cotillion finery to save an elderly man's life? I'm guessing your platoon would have traded you to the Viet Cong for that day's baseball scores. And then the Viet Cong would have used you as a human shield. I mean a literal shield, of course. Not a deterrent or anything, because ... seriously ... come on.

Anyway, I sincerely hope your bone spurs have healed. That must have been quite a burden all these years. It's like you're the Elephant Man, but without the gravitas. You are not an animal! Or a human, for that matter. Vegetable? Closer. I *know* you're not the very model of a modern major general. I'll have to think about it some more.

Love,
Pennyfarthing

◆ ◆ ◆

December 28, 2018

- Trump tweets, "We will be forced to close the Southern Border entirely if the Obstructionist Democrats do not give us the money to finish the Wall & also change the ridiculous immigration laws that our Country is saddled with. Hard to believe there was a Congress & President who would approve!"

December 29, 2018

- Trump tweets, "Any deaths of children or others at

the Border are strictly the fault of the Democrats and their pathetic immigration policies that allow people to make the long trek thinking they can enter our country illegally. They can't. If we had a Wall, they wouldn't even try! The two..... children in question were very sick before they were given over to Border Patrol. The father of the young girl said it was not their fault, he hadn't given her water in days. Border Patrol needs the Wall and it will all end. They are working so hard & getting so little credit!"

December 30, 2018

- In an interview with *The Los Angeles Times*, outgoing Chief of Staff John Kelly admits that Trump's wall is not really a wall: "The president still says 'wall' — oftentimes frankly he'll say 'barrier' or 'fencing,' now he's tended toward steel slats. But we left a solid concrete wall early on in the administration, when we asked people what they needed and where they needed it."

From the Desk of Aldous J. Pennyfarthing
To: Donald Trump, Great Wall of 'Gina

Dear Fucking Moron,

"Build the steel slats, or barrier, or fencing, or Japanese paper-and-bamboo shōji, or beaded curtain*, or earthen berm, or stretched length of piano wire, or phalanx of imaginary scarecrows, or berserking army of White House interns with pointy sticks!"

"Who's going to pay for it?!"

"After dithering for two years while holding the White House and a congressional majority, Republicans will continue to sit on their hands while the House reverts to Democratic control, and then congressional Democrats will refuse to appropriate any funds for the wall that Mexico was supposed to pay for, and then you'll force a lengthy shutdown before backing down in the face of public pressure, and you'll look like a feckless dipshit, and no one will have the stomach for another shutdown, and the wall project will languish, putrefy, and settle into the loam of the earth like your molted, scabrous simulacrum of a human skin!!!!!!!!!"

"I CAN'T HEAR YOU!!!"

"Build the steel slats, or barrier, or fencing, or Japanese paper-and-bamboo shōji, or beaded curtain, or earthen berm ..."

And so on into ∞.

-fin-

*h/t Pelosi the Great

Love,
Pennyfarthing

◆ ◆ ◆

December 31, 2019

- Trump tweets, "Remember this. Throughout the ages some things NEVER get better and NEVER change. You have Walls and you have Wheels. It was ALWAYS that way and it will ALWAYS be that way! Please explain to the Democrats that there can NEVER be a replacement for a good old fashioned WALL!"

January 1, 2019

- Trump tweets, "HAPPY NEW YEAR TO EVERYONE, INCLUDING THE HATERS AND THE FAKE NEWS MEDIA! 2019 WILL BE A FANTASTIC YEAR FOR THOSE NOT SUFFERING FROM TRUMP DERANGEMENT SYNDROME. JUST CALM DOWN AND ENJOY THE RIDE, GREAT THINGS ARE HAPPENING FOR OUR COUNTRY!"
- In a *Washington Post* op-ed, former Republican presidential nominee Mitt Romney writes, "On balance, [Trump's] conduct over the past two years ... is evidence that the president has not risen to the mantle of the office."
- Patrick Shanahan, a former Boeing executive with no military experience, becomes acting defense secretary.

January 2, 2019

- In a *New York Times* interview, former Senate Majority Leader Harry Reid says Trump is "without question the worst president we've ever had."
- The Hill reports that a lawyer for five immigrant women who worked at Trump's Bedminster, New Jersey, golf club believes "a very high number" of workers at the club were undocumented.
- While discussing border security with his cabinet, Trump says, "I know more about drones than anybody."

From the Desk of Aldous J. Pennyfarthing
To: Donald Trump, No. 1 Super-Best Science Human

Dear Fucking Moron,

You know more about drones than anybody.

Uh…

I believe you know more about *droning* than anybody, but drones?

This is just something you say when any topic comes up, right? Now I really want to finagle my way into the audience for one of the 2020 debates so I can ask the candidates their opinion on climatology, the Fed and its role in setting monetary policy, the Hadron Superconducting Supercollider, and Stormy Daniels' vagina. Your reflexive response will be, well, you know …

Or I'll just ask you about drones. Because I'm *really* interested in what you know about them — other than that you're breathlessly waiting for the day when they're sophisticated enough to bring you Diet Cokes so you can finally shitcan your chief of staff.

Seriously, though.

You know more about drones than anybody.

Ya know, I'm just gonna give you the benefit of the doubt on this one because … why the fuck not?

Love,
Pennyfarthing

January 3, 2019

- Nancy Pelosi is elected speaker of the House.

January 4, 2019

- Trump tweets, "How do you impeach a president who has won perhaps the greatest election of all time, done nothing wrong (no Collusion with Russia, it was the Dems that Colluded), had the most successful first two years of any president, and is the most popular Republican in party history 93%?"
- CNN reports that hundreds of TSA screeners, working without pay because of the government shutdown, have called out sick from major airports.

January 8, 2019

- Following Trump's assertion that "some" ex-presidents told him they should have built a border wall when they were in office, *The Washington Post* contacts spokespeople for all living former presidents and George H.W. Bush and discovers Trump was lying: "There are only four living ex-presidents. *The Washington Post* reached out to them to see whether they ever told Trump that a border wall should have been built before he was in office: All said they hadn't. A spokesman for George H.W. Bush declined to comment."
- Trump addresses the nation from the Oval Office in a last, desperate attempt to end the shutdown and get his wall. A Quinnipiac University poll later reveals that the speech convinced only 2 percent of Americans to change their mind (and doesn't specify whether they were more apt to agree or disagree with

the pr*sident).

January 9, 2019

- Trump tweets, "Billions of dollars are sent to the State of California for Forrest [sic] fires that, with proper Forrest [sic] Management, would never happen. Unless they get their act together, which is unlikely, I have ordered FEMA to send no more money. It is a disgraceful situation in lives & money!"
- Trump storms out of a meeting with Nancy Pelosi and Chuck Schumer after Pelosi says she won't agree to any funding for Trump's wall. Schumer responds, "Again, we saw a temper tantrum because he couldn't get his way."

January 10, 2019

- After a reporter asks Trump if the buck stops with him over the shutdown, Trump says, "The buck stops with everybody."

January 12, 2019

- *The Washington Post* reports that Trump "has gone to extraordinary lengths to conceal details of his conversations with Russian President Vladimir Putin, including on at least one occasion taking possession of the notes of his own interpreter and instructing the linguist not to discuss what had transpired with other administration officials."

- Two days after traveling to Texas, Trump says, "I haven't actually left the White House in months."

From the Desk of Aldous J. Pennyfarthing
To: Donald Trump, lying sack of shite

Dear Fucking Moron,

You realize we can see you, right? Fermented Diet Coke backwash is not an invisibility potion.

Let's just revisit something you said on the campaign trail, okay, Punky Brewster?

> "In this journey, I will never lie to you. I will never tell you something I do not believe."

Now this ...

> "I haven't actually left the White House in months."

And again ...

> "In this journey, I will never lie to you. I will never tell you something I do not believe."

> ...

> "I haven't actually left the White House in months."

One more time for the dotty fucktrumpets in the red hats ...

> "In this journey, I will never lie to you. I will never tell you something I do not believe."

> ...

> "I haven't actually left the White House in months."

CTRL-ALT-DELETE

Hard Reboot

{Blue Screen of Death}

YOU WERE IN TEXAS TWO DAYS AGO, YOU SEMI-AMBULA-TORY JUG OF WALRUS TALLOW! WE ALL FUCKING SAW YOU! THAT DIPSHIT HAT. THOSE DARTING, BALEFUL ORBS OF PURE INSENSATE EVIL. THAT WAS *YOU*, MOTHERFUCKER!

Don't tell me you have a body double now because ... ugh ... that poor guy. Personally, I'd let an apprentice vet tech graft a gonorrheal fruit bat to my head before I'd ever let a plastic surgeon give me your ghastly anus mouth, much less the rest of that funhouse-mirror carny booth you call a head.

Anyway, if you don't have a body double or a nifty new holograph machine, then I guess that was a ... lie?

Hmm. I'll have to think about that one.

...

Yup, it was a lie.

Love,
Pennyfarthing

◆ ◆ ◆

January 13, 2019

- Trump shares a video of Elizabeth Warren and tweets, "If Elizabeth Warren, often referred to by me as Pocahontas, did this commercial from Bighorn or Wounded Knee instead of her kitchen, with her husband dressed in full Indian garb, it would have been a smash!"

◆ ◆ ◆

January 14, 2019

- Trump serves the national champion Clemson Tigers football team cold fast food in the White House. Trump says he paid for the spread because much of the White House kitchen staff was on furlough.

◆ ◆ ◆

From the Desk of Aldous J. Pennyfarthing
To: Donald Trump, burger clown

Dear Fucking Moron,

Dude, the Clemson football team is not a busload of fourth-graders from Manitowoc, Wisconsin, driving down to Six Flags to paint Gurnee orange with their vomit. They're world-class athletes. They don't want McDonald's. *You* want McDonald's.

Just because you eat like a toddler at a South Dakota hashish den doesn't mean everyone else does — or wants to.

And you think I'm impressed that you — a guy who claims to be worth TEN BILLION DOLLARS — shelled out a few grand for cold burgers and fries?

You've wasted tens of millions in taxpayer money on golf trips, for God's sake. Granted, if Ted Cruz had been elected he'd have spent at least that much on lime and shovels, but still. You're putting us in the hole every damn month, and you're so cheap you can't even manage a decent PR stunt.

And don't think you're a paragon of urbanity and good breeding just because you threw some Wendy's into the plebeian hog trough. I know that's haute cuisine to you, but it's rubbish to most athletes. You might as well give them a juice box and a tub of lard with sprinkles on it.

My God, you are such a perpetual embarrassment.

If you were my dad I would have hanged myself from the maternity ward ceiling fan with my own umbilical cord.

Love,
Pennyfarthing

January 15, 2019

- In a newly released excerpt from his upcoming book, former New Jersey Gov. Chris Christie says Trump told him wearing a long tie makes you look thinner.

January 17, 2019

- After Nancy Pelosi recommends that Trump's State of the Union speech be postponed until after the government shutdown is ended, Trump retaliates by canceling her planned delegation to Belgium and Afghanistan. Pelosi's chief of staff tweets, "In Brussels, the delegation was scheduled to meet with top NATO commanders, U.S. military leaders and key allies — to affirm the United States' ironclad commitment to the NATO alliance."

January 19, 2019

- Trump tweets, ".@newtgingrich just stated that there has been no president since Abraham Lincoln who has been treated worse or more unfairly by the media than your favorite President, me! At the same time there has been no president who has accomplished more in his first two years in office!"

◆ ◆ ◆

January 21, 2019

- *The Washington Post* reports that Trump made 8,158 false or misleading claims during his first two years in office.
- *The Washington Post* reports on former White House aide Cliff Sims' new book, *Team of Vipers*. Among the eye-opening revelations: "At times, Trump evinced less rage than a lack of interest. Sims recounts one time when [Paul] Ryan was in the Oval Office explaining the ins and outs of the Republican health-care bill to the president. As Ryan droned on for 15 minutes, Trump sipped on a glass of Diet Coke, peered out at the Rose Garden, stared aimlessly at the walls and, finally, walked out."
- Gizmodo reports that it has found pictures on Trump's social media platforms that have been retouched to make him look thinner and make his fingers appear longer.
- On MLK Day, Trump makes an impromptu visit to the Martin Luther King Jr. Memorial, stays for about 90 seconds, and never mentions King.

◆ ◆ ◆

From the Desk of Aldous J. Pennyfarthing
To: Donald Trump, civil blight

Dear Fucking Moron,

Ninety seconds, huh?

Hope it didn't cut too much into your tweeting time, because how else will people know if a bloody-faced Mika Brzezinski is begging to get into Mar-a-Lago? Our nation turns its lonely eyes to you.

Seriously, though, you should have stayed at least five minutes. And it wouldn't have hurt to bring a black person with you. I hear Frederick Douglass was champing at the bit to go. Even, I don't know, Todd Bridges would have been a gesture of good-will.

So here's what I think happened:

You were waiting for the latest issue of *Seventeen* magazine to come in the mail, and when it didn't show up you realized there was no mail that day, and you asked your chief of staff why, and he said it's Martin Luther King Jr. Day, and you said, "Who?" and he said "the iconic and beloved civil rights leader?" and you said, "Oh, yeah, that guy," and someone shrieked, "You didn't plan anything?!?!" and you said, "Oh, sorry, what can I do that won't require much exercise and will be over before *Judge Judy* starts?" and someone else said, "You and Mike Pence should go to the MLK memorial," and you said, "Him? He's fucking creepy, and I think he 'accidentally' touched my penis once when I was in an Adderall fugue," except you didn't say "fugue" because you don't know what the fuck that means, and then you laid a wreath at the memorial and stood there for the exact amount of time you lie next to porn stars after spawning like a dying carp — you know, because you wanted to make it look good, but it didn't look good at all, it looked pathetic. And then you went home and masturbated to your sophomore college yearbook photo.

How close am I?

Love,
Pennyfarthing

◆ ◆ ◆

January 22, 2019

- The Supreme Court rules, 5-4, that Trump can continue to limit transgender soldiers' participation in the military, pending unresolved lawsuits.
- Trump tweets, "The reason Sarah Sanders does not go to the 'podium' much anymore is that the press covers her so rudely & inaccurately, in particular certain members of the press. I told her not to bother, the word gets out anyway! Most will never cover us fairly & hence, the term, Fake News!"

January 23, 2019

- After Trump insists he'll go ahead with his scheduled State of the Union speech, Nancy Pelosi shuts him down, writing, "[T]he House of Representatives will not consider a concurrent resolution authorizing the president's State of the Union address in the House chamber until government has opened."

January 25, 2019

- Former Trump campaign adviser Roger Stone is indicted on charges of witness tampering, obstruction, and giving false statements.
- After insisting he would never back down in the government shutdown stalemate with congressional Democrats, Trump agrees to open the government until February 15. He receives no money for his wall. During his speech announcing an end to the shutdown, Trump also says, "We do not need 2,000 miles

of concrete wall from sea to shining sea. We never proposed that."

From the Desk of Aldous J. Pennyfarthing
To: Donald Trump, Captain Caveman

Dear Fucking Moron,

Wow, I hope Nancy Pelosi at least grants you visitation rights to your balls. Does every other weekend sound fair?

I've never seen anyone cave that hard before. Did a giant methane bubble explode inside you or something?

And that speech! How did that feel? That's the first time I've never seen someone stand up at a podium for 20 minutes and eat shit like it was crème brûlée. You were amazingly adroit at that. Bravo!

By the way, not sure if you noticed, but Ann Coulter is not happy with you:

> "Good news for George Herbert Walker Bush: As of today, he is no longer the biggest wimp ever to serve as President of the United States."

Ouch. So you shut down the government for 35 days, destroying lives and livelihoods in the process, and have nothing to show for it. And now Ann Coulter's Adam's apple is sounding off 24/7 like a bell clapper at Notre Dame Cathedral.

Have those Moscow prostitutes contacted you yet demanding their urine back? It was obviously wasted on you. No one could ever do a better job at humiliating you than you.

Face it, this shutdown is gonna stick to you like white on Mike Pence. Your base is shrinking faster than your tapeworm-addled brain.

Love,
Pennyfarthing

January 27, 2019

- Acting White House Chief of Staff Mick Mulvaney says Trump is prepared to shut the government down again if he doesn't get a deal he likes on border security.

January 28, 2019

- An ABC/*Washington Post* poll reveals that 48 percent of Americans have no confidence at all in Trump.
- Trump tweets, "In the beautiful Midwest, windchill temperatures are reaching minus 60 degrees, the coldest ever recorded. In coming days, expected to get even colder. People can't last outside even for minutes. What the hell is going on with Global Waming [sic]? Please come back fast, we need you!

From the Desk of Aldous J. Pennyfarthing
To: Donald Trump, weather churl

Dear Fucking Moron,

Needless to say, I'd be more inclined to accept your layman's interpretation of complex global weather phenomena if you could spell them.

Write this 1,000 times on your left moob: "Weather is not climate; weather is not climate; weather is not climate." On your right moob? I don't know. Fucking tattoo *The Great Gatsby* on there or something. It's a pretty slim book. It'll fit.

Think of it this way: Right now your cholesterol is 150,000. Sometime after your heart explodes inside your chest like a Hot Pocket left in an office microwave for too long, your cholesterol will be zero. That's very low, but that doesn't mean you're healthy or that the problem will have magically resolved itself. It just means that stores will have a hard time keeping champagne, party hats, and Roman candles in stock for a while.

What the fuck was I talking about?

Oh, yeah. Global "Waming."

You spelled that wrong.

Also, Google "semicolon." Then stare at the guidelines for its proper usage for about 15 minutes while a team of tenured university climatologists take turns stapling your dick to a spastic antelope.

And never mind about your diet. I was just kidding. I'm not concerned.

Love,
Pennyfarthing

◆ ◆ ◆

January 30, 2019

- After U.S. intelligence officials publicly refute Trump on several issues, including the threat from Iran, Trump tweets, "The Intelligence people seem to be extremely passive and naive when it comes to the dangers of Iran. They are wrong! ... They are testing

Rockets (last week) and more, and are coming very close to the edge. There [sic] economy is now crashing, which is the only thing holding them back. Be careful of Iran. Perhaps Intelligence should go back to school!"

- White House Press Secretary Sarah Huckabee Sanders tells the Christian Broadcasting Network, "I think God calls all of us to fill different roles at different times and I think that He wanted Donald Trump to become president, and that's why he's there."

◆ ◆ ◆

From the Desk of Aldous J. Pennyfarthing
To: Donald Trump, dung-redolent piss-plonker

Dear Fucking Moron,

So Sarah Huckabee Sanders thinks The Good Lord made you president. Which, by extension, means He made Scott Pruitt EPA director ... to safeguard the transcendent, ineffable, surpassing beauty of Mother Earth — His prized creation. Which is a little like being president-director of the Louvre and hiring an incontinent lungfish to restore all the Renaissance paintings. But, you know, God must have His reasons.

It does make a lot of sense, because when I think of God's chosen one, the very next image that comes to mind is a guy who's the perfect synthesis of the seven deadly sins and a seven-layer burrito.

Still, I'm a bit skeptical. Mainly because you're, well, you.

Let me just try to sort this out in my infinitely puny, ungodly brain. According to the Mouth of Sauron, instead of someone we could all look up to, God chose as his prophet a serial adulterer, shameless fraudster, slovenly vulgarian, tax cheat, vainglorious layabout, indiscriminate liar, and sociopathic narcissist.

So basically what she's saying is God wanted someone who wasn't black this time.

I guess it's true that we all tend to make God in our own image, huh?

Love,
Pennyfarthing

January 31, 2019

- Trump tweets, "Democrats are becoming the Party of late term abortion, high taxes, Open Borders and Crime!"
- In an interview with *The New York Times*, Trump says, "I lost massive amounts of money doing this job."

February 1, 2019

- Trump suggests he may declare a national emergency in order to get his wall: "I think there's a good chance that we'll have to do that," he says.

February 2, 2019

- An unnamed senior White House official tells *The New York Times* that the reason for Trump's unique skin tone is "good genes."
- *Time* reports that several intelligence officials are deeply concerned about Trump's foreign policy ignorance: "Citing multiple in-person episodes, these

intelligence officials say Trump displays what one called 'willful ignorance' when presented with analyses generated by America's $81 billion-a-year intelligence services. The officials, who include analysts who prepare Trump's briefs and the briefers themselves, describe futile attempts to keep his attention by using visual aids, confining some briefing points to two or three sentences, and repeating his name and title as frequently as possible."

February 5, 2019

- Trump uses his State of the Union address to beg Democrats not to investigate him: "If there is going to be peace and legislation, there cannot be war and investigation," he says.
- Trump tweets, "Tremendous numbers of people are coming up through Mexico in the hopes of flooding our Southern Border. We have sent additional military. We will build a Human Wall if necessary. If we had a real Wall, this would be a non-event!"

From the Desk of Aldous J. Pennyfarthing
To: Donald Trump, borderline personality

Dear Fucking Moron,

A human wall? That's a great idea. Your ass alone could probably cover New Mexico and a significant portion of Arizona. Then we just need to find a billion or so other people who don't have anything better to do to block off the rest of the border.

You are a *super* genius.

Still, that Hands Across America thing didn't really work. Lots of gaps. And people need potty breaks. Somehow, I don't think you've thought this through.

Okay, I suppose you're referring to the military. Yeah, that's a good use of their time and resources. You know, "Remember the Alamo" doesn't mean Texans are actually worried that Santa Anna's troops are coming back. Of course, protracted trench warfare against kids in dirty diapers would give new meaning to the phrase "in the shit."

Somehow I think this is all just a scheme to turn immigrants into POWs so you can put them to work at your golf resorts without having to pay them minimum wage.

Many people are saying this, believe me.

Prove me wrong.

Love,
Pennyfarthing

◆ ◆ ◆

February 6, 2019

- Fact-checkers call out Trump's grotesque lie about late-term abortions from his State of the Union address.

From the Desk of Aldous J. Pennyfarthing
To: Donald Trump, Mister Fannyflaps McGee

Dear Fucking Moron,

Could you be any more full of shit?

Honestly, you'd be better off giving a State of the Bunion speech, but you hewed to tradition and gave a SOTU.

And you said this:

> "Lawmakers in New York cheered with delight upon the passage of legislation that would allow a baby to be ripped from the mother's womb moments before birth. ... And then, we had the case of the governor of Virginia where he stated he would execute a baby after birth."

First of all, before you decided to run for president as a Republican, you thought infanticide was a handy spray Home Depot stocked next to the wood mulch in the garden center. If it somehow turns out you've never paid for an abortion, I'll eat my own ass with an olive fork.

Secondly, bullshit.

Thank God for Glenn Kessler, that's all I have to say:

> "The legislation in New York would not have 'allowed a baby to be ripped from the mother's womb moments before birth.' It states that a health-care practitioner 'may perform an abortion when, according to the practitioner's reasonable and good faith professional judgment based on the facts of the patient's case: the patient is within twenty-four weeks from the commencement of pregnancy, or there is an absence of fetal viability, or the abortion is necessary to protect the patient's life or health.'"

Also ...

> "Virginia Gov. Ralph Northam (D) was widely criticized for his comments on the bill after he told a radio show that the procedures are 'done in cases where there may be severe deformities. There may

be a fetus that's not viable. So in this particular example, if a mother's in labor, I can tell you exactly what would happen. The infant would be delivered, the infant would be kept comfortable, the infant would be resuscitated if that's what the mother and the family desired. And then a discussion would ensue between the physicians and the mother.' Critics suggested the governor was endorsing infanticide. His office later said the governor was referring to medical treatment, not ending the life of a baby."

Yeah, but why worry about women's lives or families' ability to make excruciatingly difficult choices on their own terms when there are political points to be had?

At long last, have you no sense of decency?

Love,
Pennyfarthing

◆ ◆ ◆

February 7, 2019

- Trump tweets, "PRESIDENTIAL HARASSMENT! It should never be allowed to happen again!"

◆ ◆ ◆

February 8, 2019

- *Vanity Fair* quotes a former West Wing official as saying, "Trump is hated by everyone inside the White House."

◆ ◆ ◆

February 9, 2019

- Trump tweets, "We have a great economy DESPITE the Obama Administration and all of its job killing Regulations and Roadblocks. If that thinking prevailed in the 2016 Election, the U.S. would be in a Depression right now! We were heading down, and don't let the Democrats sound bites fool you!" For the record, Obama inherited a deep recession from Republican George W. Bush and turned the economy around, creating millions of jobs each year after the downturn ended. On most measures, including jobs, the gains in the economy under Trump have simply been a continuation of those achieved under Obama. Obama also presided over a near tripling of the S&P 500.
- After an Axios report reveals that Trump spends an insane amount of his workday in unstructured "executive time," the administration attempts to hunt down the person who leaked the pr*sident's schedules.

◆ ◆ ◆

From the Desk of Aldous J. Pennyfarthing
To: Donald Trump, couch yam

Dear Fucking Moron,

Okay, so I took a peek at your daily itinerary. Honestly, my expectations for you are so low at this point, the only surprise was that your chief of staff doesn't block off three hours for a daily hose-down in the National Zoo rhino paddock.

Seriously, this doesn't sound like a president so much as William Randolph Hearst after he had a stroke:

> "[H]e spends his mornings in the residence, watching TV, reading the papers, and responding to what

he sees and reads by phoning aides, members of Congress, friends, administration officials and informal advisers."

Get off your lazy, goldbricking ass, you gluttonous sluggard. You have a country to run into the ground.

And now you're sending your flying monkeys out to find the leaker? Wait, here's a thought: Maybe don't have a schedule that would make a preschooler roll her eyes and mutter "must be nice."

You know, I wouldn't mind the TV watching so much if you picked something a bit more intellectually stimulating … like, I don't know, *The Newlywed Game*. But you watch *Fox & Friends*, which is like news for people with gaping, untreated head wounds. I mean, Brian Kilmeade is essentially a waxed ape with an undiagnosed foot of rebar stuck in his skull. And I wouldn't hire Steve Doocy if I had an opening for a full-time paint huffer.

Jesus Christ, get a real job.

Hopefully your interns know what the fuck they're doing at least.

Love,
Pennyfarthing

February 11, 2019

- El Paso city officials issue a resolution calling on Trump to stop spreading the lie that the city was awash in crime before the government erected a fence: "The County of El Paso is disillusioned by President Trump's lies regarding the border and our community, and though it is difficult to welcome him to El Paso while he continues to proliferate such untruths, we do welcome him to meet with local officials to become properly informed about our great and safe region."

February 12, 2019

- At a rally, Trump says he wouldn't mind having a dog, but he doesn't have the time. Dogs everywhere rejoice.

February 14, 2019

- William Barr is confirmed as attorney general.
- *60 Minutes* host Scotty Pelley reveals that former Acting FBI Director Andrew McCabe told him there had been discussions at the Justice Department about removing Trump under the 25th Amendment.

February 15, 2019

- Trump declares a national emergency in order to fund his border wall. During his announcement, he inadvertently admits there's no emergency, saying, "I didn't need to do this, but I'd rather do it much faster."
- Just hours after declaring a national emergency, Trump flies to Mar-a-Lago.

From the Desk of Aldous J. Pennyfarthing
To: Donald Trump, the *real* national emergency

Dear Fucking Moron,

So why would a president fly to a resort for a golf weekend just hours after declaring a national emergency?

I can think of only two reasons.

1. It's not a real emergency
2. He's not a real president

The correct answer? Both 1 and 2, of course.

Ah, yes, the boy who cried "golf" strikes again. This is like calling the fire department to hose down your patio furniture, for fuck's sake.

"I didn't need to do this, but I'd rather do it much faster."

Nice one, Barry Zuckerkorn. You could have taken a shit in your hand, dressed it up as a *Downton Abbey* under-butler, and sang the libretto from *Carmen* to it and it wouldn't have undermined your credibility nearly as much as *that* little truth bomb.

You pick the weirdest times to accidentally tell the truth, Machia-jelly. If only you'd done so during your inauguration:

> JOHN ROBERTS: "Repeat after me. I, Donald John Trump, do solemnly swear that I will faithfully execute the office of president of the United States, and will to the best of my ability, preserve, protect and defend the Constitution of the United States."
>
> YOU: "Yeah, I'm not going to do any of that. Fuck you, Roberts. Reince! Nacho cheese sauce! I'm parched! Hit me!"

And what if we have an *actual* emergency? How many times can you send the Marines to the Albuquerque Orange Julius for an urgent ball-scratching mission before they just stop showing up?

I hate to break it to you, but the national emergency is that the RAM in your head is 90 percent devoted to running Flying Toasters and 9 percent focused on remembering the names of porn actresses, which leaves just 1 percent for obsessively hitting your Diet Coke button like a lab rat jonesing for cocaine pellets.

Love,
Pennyfarthing

February 17, 2019

- Two days after Trump reveals Japanese Prime Minister Shinzo Abe nominated him for a Nobel Peace Prize, the Japanese newspaper *Asahi Shimbun* reports Abe did indeed nominate him ... at the request of the White House. Trump had earlier claimed, "Prime Minister Abe of Japan gave me the most beautiful copy of a letter that he sent to the people who give out a thing called the Nobel Prize. ... You know why? Because he had rocket ships and he had missiles flying over Japan. They feel safe. I did that."

◆ ◆ ◆

From the Desk of Aldous J. Pennyfarthing
To: Donald Trump, Asian turd flu

Dear Fucking Moron,

Say, do you have Shinzo Abe's number? I'm hoping he'll nominate me for a Grammy for my latest spoken word album, *Screams From My Toilet*. I think I have a real chance this time!

And, hey, you could win that Nobel Prize thing, too. Then

again, I could start firing Krugerrands from my left nipple like a Pez dispenser. As I've previously noted, in an infinite number of parallel universes, everything is bound to happen at least once. Which means there's gotta be at least one universe in which Carrot Top is president. Which also means I'm going to spend pretty much the rest of my life searching for wormholes to other realities in people's wardrobes, because that universe sounds way, *way* better.

Or maybe I'll travel to the universe where I'm head of the Nobel Committee and then give all the prizes to *me*. I'll get the Nobel in Physics for discovering wormholes, of course, and the Nobel Peace Prize for telling you to go fuck yourself 'cause ain't no way you gettin' any fuckin' Nobels, Pancake Larry.

Love,
Pennyfarthing

◆ ◆ ◆

February 18, 2019

- Sixteen states sue Trump over his national emergency declaration.

◆ ◆ ◆

February 19, 2019

- *The Washington Post* reports, "Several current and former Trump administration appointees promoted sales of nuclear power plants to Saudi Arabia despite repeated objections from members of the National Security Council and other senior White House officials, according to a new report from congressional Democrats."
- Trump tweets, "Had the opposition party (no, not the

Media) won the election, the Stock Market would be down at least 10,000 points by now. We are heading up, up, up!" Again, the S&P 500 nearly tripled under Obama.

◆ ◆ ◆

February 20, 2019

- The government announces that a Coast Guard lieutenant was planning a terrorist attack targeting journalists and politicians in order to "establish a white homeland." His hit list included Nancy Pelosi, Joe Scarborough, Alexandria Ocasio-Cortez, and "Sen blumen jew" (Sen. Richard Blumenthal). All are frequent Trump targets. Trump takes two days to comment on the news, saying, "I think it's a shame." Asked whether he thinks he bears any responsibility for the planned attack, Trump says, "I think my language is very nice."
- Trump tweets, "The New York Times reporting is false. They are a true ENEMY OF THE PEOPLE!"

◆ ◆ ◆

February 21, 2019

- U.S. District Judge Kenneth Marra rules that Labor Secretary Alexander Acosta broke the law when he gave Jeffrey Epstein a sweetheart plea deal that allowed the accused pedophile to serve only 13 months for allegedly sexually abusing dozens of underage girls.

◆ ◆ ◆

February 23, 2019

- During a televised Oval Office meeting, a Chinese official audibly laughs as Trump and U.S. Trade Representative Robert Lighthizer contradict each other on trade policy.

February 24, 2019

- Trump tweets, "HOLD THE DATE! We will be having one of the biggest gatherings in the history of Washington, D.C., on July 4th. It will be called 'A Salute To America' and will be held at the Lincoln Memorial. Major fireworks display, entertainment and an address by your favorite President, me!"

From the Desk of Aldous J. Pennyfarthing
To: Donald Trump, Benedict Arnold Ziffel

Dear Fucking Moron,

Wow. You really *have* accomplished more than any other president. Only a genius as geniusy as Donald J. Trump would ever think of having a Fourth of July party on the Fourth of July. And you're going to salute *America*? Where do you come up with this stuff?

Thanks for the reminder, though. Luckily that's Geraldo's birthday, so I'd already asked for the day off. But some losers and haters might not have thought that far ahead.

Say, I need your advice. I was thinking of hosting a bris for a 96-year-old Japanese woman. I was hoping to have fireworks and a bouncy house resembling a giant, marginally hygienic foreskin. Good idea? Bad idea? Aw, man. It sucks, doesn't it? I just don't have your feel for this sort of thing. I mean, I'm talking to the guy who came up with the Fourth of July Fourth of July party. You're a legend, dude.

Anyway, I will definitely HOLD THE DATE! No need to tell me a second time. Though, come to think of it, maybe you could send out a reminder when the day gets closer. I definitely *do not* want to miss another seven-hour speech about your Electoral College map.

Thanks, man.

Love,
Pennyfarthing

February 25, 2019

> • Alva Johnson, a former Trump campaign staffer, says Trump kissed her on the lips without permission. In an interview with MSNBC's Chris Hayes, Johnson later said the incident was just like what was described in the *Access Hollywood* tape: "When I heard audio, I was like screaming in my car. I'm like, oh my God, that's exactly what he did to me. He literally described exactly what he did to me, minus the grab the 'P.'"

◆ ◆ ◆

From the Desk of Aldous J. Pennyfarthing
To: Donald Trump, Grabby McGrabhands

Dear Fucking Moron,

First of all, kudos to Ms. Johnson for not vomiting her small intestines the moment your tree fungus skin came within Taser range of her lips.

But, seriously, you're still doing this shit? You're a gross old man, dude. Your lips look like a couple of earthworms that got stranded on a hot sidewalk. You make the Notre Dame Cathedral gargoyles look fuckable. You're what you'd get if Steve Bannon took a tab of Orange Sunshine and fucked a roast beef sandwich. If I ever get an erection again after seeing your Hieronymus Bosch oil painting of a head it will be such an otherworldly, numinous miracle the church will use it to canonize Larry Flynt.

Also, it doesn't really *matter* whether or not you're an upchuck-inducing bridge troll. Even if you looked like George Clooney it would be *fucking inappropriate*. It's not 1961. Have you ever watched *Mad Men*? It's not a tutorial, for fuck's sake.

As they say, absolute power corrupts absolutely, even if — or *especially* if — you look like a bag of petrified lipo fat.

Love,
Pennyfarthing

February 27, 2019

- While Trump rests his bone spurs in Vietnam, former Trump lawyer and fixer Michael Cohen testifies before the House Oversight Committee.

◆ ◆ ◆

From the Desk of Aldous J. Pennyfarthing
To: Donald Trump, racist cheating conman

Dear Fucking Moron,

Holy Fish-slappin' Christ, did you see that hearing?

Michael Cohen really said a lot of mean things about you. I haven't seen a sidekick fuck his hero this vigorously since I wrote, directed, produced, distributed, marketed, and made a nonspeaking eight-second cameo in that Batman and Robin porno.

That must have hurt. If you had blood, I bet it would be boiling right now. (What *is* running through your veins, by the way? For some reason I've always pictured millions of tiny black spiders kayaking down a barmy river of McRib sauce. But that can't be right.)

Anyway, here's just a portion of his testimony:

> "I am ashamed that I chose to take part in concealing Mr. Trump's illicit acts rather than listening to my own conscience.

> "I am ashamed because I know what Mr. Trump is.

> "He is a racist.

> "He is a conman.

> "He is a cheat."

And *this* story. Ugh:

> "Mr. Trump is a racist. The country has seen Mr. Trump court white supremacists and bigots. You have heard him call poorer countries 'shitholes.'

> "In private, he is even worse.

> "He once asked me if I could name a country run by a black person that wasn't a 'shithole.' This was when Barack Obama was president of the United States.

> "While we were once driving through a struggling neighborhood in Chicago, he commented that only black people could live that way.

"And he told me that black people would never vote for him because they were too stupid."

Wow. You're an incorrigible fucking racist! Who knew?

There's a lot more, including allegations that you may have been involved in tax fraud, wire fraud, bank fraud, campaign finance law violations, suborning of perjury, conspiracy, etc.

Then again, Michael Cohen *is* a convicted liar. Whom you kept on your payroll for more than 10 years. So at best you have really, really shitty judgment when it comes to trusting pathological liars.

Glad you're in Vietnam meeting with Kim Jong Un right now. I can't even imagine what could go wrong.

Love,
Pennyfarthing

February 28, 2019

- Fordham University confirms it once received a threatening letter from Trump's team demanding the school not release Trump's academic records.
- *The New York Times* reports that Trump ordered his chief of staff, John Kelly, to give Jared Kushner a security clearance, despite a recommendation from intelligence officials that he not receive one. The report contradicted Trump's earlier assertion that he'd had no role in his son-in-law's receiving the clearance.
- The U.S.-North Korea summit ends with no deal or agreement. Regarding U.S. citizen Otto Warmbier, who died shortly after being returned to the U.S. from North Korean custody (presumably as a result of brutal treatment on the part of Kim Jong Un's govern-

ment), Trump defends Kim, saying, "He tells me he didn't know about it, and I take him at his word."

From the Desk of Aldous J. Pennyfarthing
To: Donald Trump, Pacific Rim job

Dear Fucking Moron,

So that was pretty pointless, huh? It's almost like you traveled to North Korea — in the process legitimizing Kim's draconian joke of a government and giving him boatloads of propaganda with which to mindfuck his own people — without any plan at all!

I mean, diplomacy is not like showing up at a Mediterranean food cart and deciding on the spot whether to go with the falafel or the shawarma. You're supposed to have a deal hammered out before the very busy world leaders meet.

Did you just need to get out of the house? Next time maybe do hot yoga or something. You might like it. It's like sitting in a sauna, except you've got tight pants on so your balls never hit the tile with the resounding clap of a sea lion carcass being tossed out onto a wharf.

Speaking of resounding clap, are you actually sleeping with Kim Jong Un? Because for the life of me I can't understand your solicitous behavior toward him unless you really are, as you've previously noted, in love. It's either that or the very notion of starving and brutalizing your own citizens gives you a tingle up your leg the likes of which you've never felt before.

I mean, sheesh. Who's gonna break it to Melania and whatever eight-dimensional outer-space sparkle-unicorn Dear Leader is fucking?

Next time at least bring home a souvenir for all of us. A jar of spicy kimchi might be nice.

Love,
Pennyfarthing

March 2, 2019

- Trump plugs his golf course in Scotland, tweeting, "Very proud of perhaps the greatest golf course any-where in the world. Also, furthers U.K. relationship!"
- Trump speaks at the annual Conservative Political Action Conference (CPAC).

From the Desk of Aldous J. Pennyfarthing
To: Donald Trump, verbose sock monkey

Dear Fucking Moron,

Yeah, nice Hitler boof rally, Mein Drumpf.

You spoke for more than two hours and hardly got tired — like you were supercharged, man. I felt the electricity, too! Like John Bolton had attached the jumper cables from an M1 Abrams tank battery to my balls.

But, woof! That was some word salad. Listening to one of your hours-long virtuoso larynx sharts is like trying to play Ping-Pong against a Piper Cub propeller. There's just no way to win. For *anyone*.

Not sure what my favorite part was. When you claimed California Gov. Gavin Newsom called you to say, "You're a great president and you are doing a great job"? Yeah, that totally happened.

When you mocked Jeff Sessions' Southern accent?

When you got your fans to shout "lock her up!" three days after Michael Cohen's congressional testimony implicated you in numerous alleged felonies?

Oh, I know!

This:

> "The big inauguration speech. You take a look at those crowds. And I watched one of the evening shows that are ridiculous how horrible they are, how mean, how horrible. And I watched it by mistake, and they showed, they showed from the White House all the way down, they showed from the Cap ..., they showed, there were people, nobody's ever seen it, the Capitol, down to the Washington Monument, people. But I saw pictures that, there were no people. Those pictures were taken hours before."

Let's see, right now it's approximately ... uh ... who-gives-a-flying-fuck-about-this-o-'clock. And you're *still* whining about your fucking inauguration crowds? Twenty-five-plus months later? Mein Gott im Himmel, what the fuck is wrong with you?

Maybe if you actually tried to do your job instead of lying about your media coverage you could get reelected and inspire people to show up at your *next* inauguration.

Sorry, I just vomited a lifetime's worth of movie theater Milk Duds. I'll have to cut this short.

Love,
Pennyfarthing

◆ ◆ ◆

March 3, 2019

- Trump attempts to blame Michael Cohen's congressional testimony for his failed North Korea summit, tweeting, "For the Democrats to interview in open hearings a convicted liar & fraudster, at the same time as the very important Nuclear Summit with North Korea, is perhaps a new low in American politics and may have contributed to the 'walk.' Never done when a president is overseas. Shame!"

◆ ◆ ◆

March 4, 2019

- As part of a wide-ranging investigation of Trump, congressional Democrats request documents from 81 government agencies and other groups.
- An explosive report in *The New Yorker* alleges that Trump ordered Gary Cohn, the former director of the National Economic Council, to block the AT&T Time Warner merger, presumably in order to punish his bête noire CNN and boost Fox News: "According to a well-informed source, Trump called Cohn into the Oval Office along with John Kelly, who had just become the chief of staff, and said in exasperation to Kelly, 'I've been telling Cohn to get this lawsuit filed and nothing's happened! I've mentioned it 50 times. And nothing's happened. I want to make sure it's filed. I want that deal blocked!'"

From the Desk of Aldous J. Pennyfarthing
To: Donald Trump, teevee tyrant

Dear Fucking Moron,

Is that a banana republic in your pocket or are you just Mussolini?

Good God, man. Getting criticized is the high price one pays for being president. Punishing news outlets that give you unfavorable coverage while calling them the enemy of the people is like greasing the skids for fascism with your own ass fat.

For the last fucking time, the United States is not one of your shitty casinos. You may run the country into the ground eventually, but not without resistance from other civil servants. Or uncivil servants, as the case may be.

Just try to pretend you're running an actual representative liberal democracy for once, you fusty cretin. I'm exhausted with this loutish tin-pot despotism, and for once I'd like to wake up in the morning without worrying that today's the day my asshole neighbor with the Toby Keith T-shirt and irregular earlobes gets deputized as a stormtrooper.

Love,
Pennyfarthing

❖ ❖ ❖

March 5, 2019

- The White House says it will refuse to hand over documents to congressional Democrats related to Jared Kushner's security clearance. *The New York Times* had earlier reported that Kushner received a clearance because Trump had insisted on it over intelligence officials' objections.

❖ ❖ ❖

From the Desk of Aldous J. Pennyfarthing
To: Donald Trump, Ivanka Trump starter kit

Dear Fucking Moron,

You know how I can tell you're an idiot? You think Jared Kushner is smart.

It boggles my mind that the same people who conveniently ignore the fact that Jared Kushner (who will totally bring peace to the Middle East just as soon as he finishes the maze on his Applebee's placemat) appears to be running the country think people like Nancy Pelosi don't belong in Congress.

Maybe, just maybe, intelligence officials know a bit more about protecting our nation than the guy who walks around 24/7 with an unsecured cellphone?

Seriously, though, this concerns me. I mean, you could have picked just about anyone for a high-ranking White House advisory role, and yet you chose Ivanka's third-favorite dildo.

The guy has the intellect of an egg salad sandwich, FFS.

When you two play Chutes and Ladders, how long does it take to explain to him that the chutes aren't just shiny ladders?

If you replaced his head with a giant wedge of Gruyère cheese, how long would it be before that head ended up in an omelet?

I don't really get how he can be this stupid, though. He runs a huge company. After you asked him to get to the bottom of the opioid crisis, did he do a little too much hands-on research?

Or maybe he's just a shitty businessman with a completely delusional sense of his own abilities and importance. Then again, he's probably smarter and savvier than *you*, which is all it takes, apparently.

So, yeah, thanks again for making me feel safe. I've got the warm fuzzies all over. Or maybe that's just radiation. I haven't checked the news wires in the past 15 minutes.

Love,
Pennyfarthing

March 6, 2019

- Trump reverses an Obama executive order requiring the U.S. to report on civilians killed in drone strikes.
- Despite Trump's monomaniacal efforts to reduce the trade deficit, it soars to a record $891 billion for the year.
- At a meeting of the American Workforce Policy Advisory Board, Trump calls Apple CEO Tim Cook "Tim Apple."

March 7, 2019

- Michael Cohen sues the Trump Organization for $1.9 million in unpaid legal fees.

March 8, 2019

- In response to a House resolution condemning hate, Trump, who once said there were "very fine people" on both sides of the Charlottesville protests, says Democrats have become "an anti-Jewish party."

- During a visit to Alabama to survey tornado damage, Trump signs Bibles for his fans.
- *The Miami Herald* reports that Trump was photographed watching the Super Bowl with the founder of the Florida spa where New England Patriots owner Robert Kraft was arrested for soliciting prostitution.

March 10, 2019

- Trump tweets, "More people are working today in the United States, 158,000,000, than at any time in our Country's history. That is a Big Deal!" He fails to mention that there are also more people in the United States than at any time in our country's history.
- Axios reports that Trump claims he didn't actually call Tim Cook "Tim Apple" four days earlier at a meeting, but rather said "Tim Cook Apple" really fast while saying the "Cook" part softly. He also reportedly said "the Democrats hate Jewish people" and told an unfunny and tasteless joke about blackface.

March 11, 2019

- Trump proposes a $4.7 trillion budget that pushes the annual deficit past $1 trillion. The budget calls for increases in military spending and steep cuts to domestic programs. Nancy Pelosi condemns the budget as a "roadmap to a sicker, weaker America."

- Trump changes his story on the Tim Cook Apple "controversy" once again, tweeting, "At a recent round table meeting of business executives, & long after formally introducing Tim Cook of Apple, I quickly referred to Tim + Apple as Tim/Apple as an easy way to save time & words. The Fake News was disparagingly all over this, & it became yet another bad Trump story!"

◆ ◆ ◆

From the Desk of Aldous J. Pennyfarthing
To: Donald Trump Grifter

Dear Fucking Moron,

You are just a big bowl of bonkers, aren't you?

So you called Tim Cook "Tim Apple" to "save time & words"? You do realize "Apple" has more syllables than "Cook," right? And …

Wait, why am I arguing with a guy whose head is basically just a Hobby Lobby piñata full of 19th century diseases and Fiddle Faddle?

GET HELP!

I mean, this is "Kim Jong Un found a unicorn"-level shit.

Come on, L'il Donnie. Every PR professional knows that your explanations are supposed to get *more* plausible, not less, as you go. And your previous excuse was fucking horrible. You said "Tim Cook Apple" really fast but said the "Cook" part softly? As if you've ever said *anything* without sounding like a jet engine sucking in a herd of ostriches.

Seriously, dude. I think there's *really* something wrong with you. Maybe take one of those online quizzes that lets you check whether you're a sociopath. I'm guessing you'll have your answer after the first two questions.

Love,
Pennyfarthing

◆ ◆ ◆

March 13, 2019

- Sounding completely sane, Trump tweets, "The Fake News photoshopped pictures of Melania, then propelled conspiracy theories that it's actually not her by my side in Alabama and other places. They are only getting more deranged with time!"
- In an interview with Breitbart News, Trump says, "You know, the left plays a tougher game, it's very funny. I actually think that the people on the right are tougher, but they don't play it tougher. Okay? I can tell you I have the support of the police, the support of the military, the support of the Bikers for Trump — I have the tough people, but they don't play it tough — until they go to a certain point, and then it would be very bad, very bad. But the left plays it cuter and tougher."

◆ ◆ ◆

March 14, 2019

- With the help of several Republican votes, the Senate passes a resolution meant to block Trump's phony national emergency declaration. After the vote, Trump tweets, "VETO!"
- After Beto O'Rourke announces his presidential run, Trump says, "Well, I think he's got a lot of hand movement. I've never seen so much hand movement. I said,

'Is he crazy or is that just the way he acts?'"

From the Desk of Aldous J. Pennyfarthing
To: Donald Trump, Texas-sized arsehole

Dear Fucking Moron,

Okay, seriously. You've never seen so much hand movement? I have a hard time believing *you* of all people don't own a mirror. Just because we need the Hubble Space Telescope to see your gnarly little gerbil hands doesn't mean they're not spastically flying around like a couple of drugged eels in a Sherwin-Williams paint mixer.

The difference between you and Beto? He doesn't move his hands around to cruelly pantomime disabled people.

And you think he might be crazy?

Ugh.

Dude, you invented crazy. Or, at the very least, you're the Goodyear radial tire to the Mesopotamians' shitty clay wheel. If you want to sue someone, sue the editors of the DSM-5 for publishing your life story without permission.

Jesus Christ, you are so exhausting. Also, Google "projection." Now Google "Donald Trump projection." Now Google "Donald Trump Teddy Ruxpin sex tape."

I'm just curious. Which one got the most hits?

Love,
Pennyfarthing

March 15, 2019

- A gunman opens fire at two mosques in New Zealand, killing 50. The killer's manifesto praises Trump as "a symbol of renewed white identity and common purpose."

◆ ◆ ◆

March 16, 2019

- Seven months after Sen. John McCain's death, Trump attacks him in a tweet: "Spreading the fake and totally discredited Dossier 'is unfortunately a very dark stain against John McCain.' Ken Starr, Former Independent Counsel. He had far worse 'stains' than this, including thumbs down on repeal and replace after years of campaigning to repeal and replace!"

◆ ◆ ◆

March 17, 2019

- Trump concludes a bizarre 24-hour Twitter bender in which he attacked not only John McCain but also a *Saturday Night Live* rerun, GM, the UAW Local 1112's president, Hillary Clinton, the Mueller investigation, Joe Biden, Andrew McCabe, Google, and many more. He also retweets a QAnon conspiracy theorist and a Pizzagate conspiracy theorist.
- For the second day in a row, Trump attacks the late Sen. John McCain on Twitter: "So it was indeed (just proven in court papers) 'last in his class' (Annapolis) John McCain that sent the Fake Dossier to the FBI and Media hoping to have it printed BEFORE the Election. He & the Dems, working together, failed (as usual). Even the Fake News refused this garbage!"

March 18, 2019

- *The New York Times* reports that Trump once significantly inflated his net worth while pursuing a loan from Deutsche Bank: "Mr. Trump told Deutsche Bank his net worth was about $3 billion, but when bank employees reviewed his finances, they concluded he was worth about $788 million, according to documents produced during a lawsuit Mr. Trump brought against the former *New York Times* journalist Timothy O'Brien. And a senior investment-banking executive said in an interview that he and others cautioned that Mr. Trump should be avoided because he had worked with people in the construction industry connected to organized crime."

March 19, 2019

- Trump again attacks the late Sen. John McCain, this time in the Oval Office: "I was never a fan of John McCain and I never will be," he says.

March 20, 2019

- Speaking to reporters outside the White House, Trump says, "I just won an election with 63 million votes or so, 63 million. I had 206 to 223 in the Electoral College, 306 to 223. And I'm saying to myself, 'Wait a minute, I just won one of the greatest elections of all time in the history of this country,' and even you will admit that, 'and now I have somebody writing a report that never got a vote. It's called the Mueller report.' So explain that, because my voters don't get it. And I don't get it."

- For the fourth time in five days, Trump attacks John McCain. During a speech "focused" on the economy, Trump says, "I have to be honest, I never liked him much. I probably never will. ... I endorsed him at his request and I gave him the kind of funeral that he wanted, which as president I had to approve. I don't care about this. I didn't get a thank-you. That's okay."

March 21, 2019

- Trump says the U.S. should recognize Israel's sovereignty over the Golan Heights, which was captured from Syria in 1967. Israel's occupation of the region has long been seen as illegal under international law.
- House Oversight Chair Elijah Cummings says Jared Kushner's lawyer told him Kushner uses the encrypted messaging app WhatsApp to send official communications. He says the recipients include foreigners.
- For the *fifth time in six days*, Trump attacks John McCain. During an interview with Fox Business Network's Maria Bartiromo, Trump says, "He was horrible with what he did with repeal and replace. What he did to the Republican Party and to the nation and to sick people who could have had great health care, was not good. So I'm not a fan of John McCain and that's fine."

From the Desk of Aldous J. Pennyfarthing
To: Donald Trump, America's "It" Ghoul

Dear Fucking Moron,

I haven't checked my Emily Post in a while, but I believe when you make grotesque, unsolicited attacks on deceased war heroes you're supposed to stop at one. Here's how you remember that: It's like what your doctor told you about eating whole pot roasts.

Seriously, you need a dental hygienist to go to work between the folds of your cerebrum with a tooth scraper and a cordless Waterpik. Because you are effing disturbed, man, and I don't think cognitive therapy will do you a whit of good. It would be like taking a couple of ibuprofen for a gunshot wound. Or for the very, very painful condition known as bone spurs. Heard of it?

John McCain has been dead for *seven months*, for the gods' sake. You can't let this go? Granted, when you die, the government will have to build a network of aqueducts to your grave to accommodate all the patriotic Americans who want to micturate upon it, but then again, you suck very-much-large-time. That's the difference. McCain was an honorable man I just happened to disagree with a lot. Whereas the movie of your life will be titled *Donald Trump: American Piss Pot*.

Get a mental checkup, Cow-ligula. It's way past time.

Love,
Pennyfarthing

March 22, 2019

- Trump tweets, "It was announced today by the U.S. Treasury that additional large scale Sanctions would be added to those already existing Sanctions on North Korea. I have today ordered the withdrawal of those additional Sanctions!"
- Trump nominates crank economist and former Trump campaign adviser Stephen Moore for a seat on the Fed's Board of Governors. Moore is the co-author of a book titled *Trumponomics*.
- Robert Mueller submits his report on 2016 Russian election interference to Attorney General William Barr.

◆ ◆ ◆

March 24, 2019

- In a letter to Congress, Attorney General William Barr gives a short summary of the Mueller Report. He states that Mueller's team "did not establish that members of the Trump campaign conspired or coordinated with the Russian government in its election interference activities." With regard to obstruction of justice, Barr writes that while the report "does not conclude that the President committed a crime, it also does not exonerate him." However, Barr says that the available evidence "is not sufficient to establish that the President committed an obstruction-of-justice offense."

From the Desk of Aldous J. Pennyfarthing

To: Donald Trump, not-exonerated person of interest

Dear Fucking Moron,

Wow, what a great day for Donnie J. Trump! Looks like you dodged a bullet there, Chachi. You're only *sort of* a crook — at least according to the letter your handpicked attorney general wrote based on a report hardly anyone has seen yet.

Congratulations!

But since the letter — which, again, apparently boils down to "we're not going to charge this shithead because there's not quite enough evidence" — clearly says that you *weren't* exonerated, I'm puzzled about what the fuck you're talking about here:

> "No Collusion, No Obstruction, Complete and Total EXONERATION. KEEP AMERICA GREAT!"

Yeah, that's kind of the opposite of what the letter said, don't you think? Then again, reading comprehension has never really been your thing.

So since the Mueller Report is so chock-full of exonerating nougaty goodness, you won't mind if we see it in its entirety without redactions, right?

Right?

Anyway, somewhere or other I got the impression that the entire Mueller investigation was a hoax. So I guess they can start the *real* investigation now, huh?

Oh, and don't spike the ball just yet. The Southern District of New York is still on the field, and they're sharpening their orange-head-stompin' cleats as we speak.

Love,
Pennyfarthing

March 25, 2019

- *The Washington Post* reports that Trump doesn't want too much money going to Puerto Rico, whose residents are U.S. citizens: "[A]t an Oval Office meeting on Feb. 22, Trump asked top advisers for ways to limit federal support from going to Puerto Rico, believing it is taking money that should be going to the mainland, according to senior administration officials who spoke on the condition of anonymity to share details of the president's private remarks."

March 26, 2019

- At a House hearing, Education Secretary Betsy DeVos attempts to defend her proposal to cut nearly $18 million in funding for the Special Olympics. "We had to make some difficult decisions with this budget," she says.
- In a legal filing, the Trump Justice Department states that it now backs striking down Obamacare in its entirety. If the administration gets its way, tens of millions of Americans will be thrown off their insurance.

March 27, 2019

- Trump throws Education Secretary Betsy DeVos under the bus with respect to Special Olympics funding, saying, "I have overridden my people" on the issue.

March 28, 2019

- Speaking with reporters on the White House lawn, Trump says, "Puerto Rico has been taken care of better by Donald Trump than by any living human being."
- At a rally in Michigan, the actual president of the United States says, "I support the Great Lakes. Always have. They are beautiful. They are big, very deep. Record deepness, right?" He also says, "If Hillary got in … you'd be doing wind. Windmills. Weeee. And if it doesn't blow, you can forget about television for that night. 'Darling, I want to watch television.' 'I'm sorry. The wind isn't blowing.' I know a lot about wind. I know a lot about wind."

March 29, 2019

- In a letter to Congress, Attorney General William Barr says a redacted version of the Mueller report will be released by mid-April.
- Trump threatens to shut down the U.S.-Mexico border if Mexico doesn't magically stop all illegal immigration into the U.S.

March 30, 2019

- Excerpts from Rick Reilly's new book *Commander in Cheat: How Golf Explains Trump* are released. In one anecdote, ESPN's Mike Tirico talks about hitting the shot of his life before walking up to the hole and seeing his ball in a bunker. "Trump's caddy came up to me and said, 'You know that shot you hit on the par 5?'" Tirico says. "'It was about 10 feet from the hole. Trump threw it in the bunker. I watched him do it.'"

◆ ◆ ◆

April 1, 2019

From the Desk of Aldous J. Pennyfarthing
To: Donald Trump, April Tool

Dear Fucking Moron,

Another year gone by, and you just keep getting worse. Honestly, I'd almost be relieved if you peeled off your skin during your next State of the Union address to reveal your menacing Sleestak face. At least the world would start to make sense again.

If we're in thrall to a race of subterranean reptiles who are experimenting on us like lab monkeys, at least we'll know we'll be taken reasonably good care of until we're chloroformed and dissected.

As it is, I can't rule out the possibility that I fell down a manhole in 2016 while playing Pokémon Go and am now in hell. This could go on literally forever.

Well, if it does, I'll just keep writing these letters ... until you learn. Which means I'll never stop writing these letters.

Which *also* means I truly am Sisyphus, pushing a boulder uphill for all eternity.

But, hey, someone has to do it.

By the way, this is your last chance to shout "April fool!" and resign like a good little boy.

No?

Fine.

See you in the funny papers, Sluggo.

Love,
Pennyfarthing

Note to my wonderful readers: I waited a year to publish this sequel, and while I was writing it, it sometimes felt like I was trying to shove 500 pounds of crazy into a 5-pound bag. Trump's insanity is accelerating — so much so that it will likely soon collapse in on itself like a gravitational singularity. So I plan to publish my next Trump-bashin' book a bit sooner next time.

Look for the third installment of the Dear F*cking [_____] series sometime in 2019.

Get active. Get involved. Get out the vote.
I mean it.

Made in the USA
Monee, IL
25 July 2020